Go and Make Disciples!

Vision for Discipleship

Revised Edition

Reuven & Yanit Ross

Go and Make Disciples!

ISBN-13: 978-1499152074, copyright © 2014
Printed in the United States of America
Printed by CreateSpace, an Amazon.com Company

Cover Photograph – Sunrise overlooking the Sea of Galilee from Tiberias

Photograph, layout, and design by Reuven Ross

Website: www.making-disciples.net
Email: reuven@making-disciples.net
        yanit@making-disciples.net

First Printing, 2000, Israel

Second Printing, 2001, Malaysia

Third Printing, 2002, USA

Fourth Printing, 2004, USA

Fifth Printing, 2007, South Africa

Sixth Printing, 2014, USA – CreateSpace

Contents

Cover Page

Copyright

Contents

Foreword 1

Getting Acquainted 2

The Purpose for a Vision of Discipleship.............................. 3

A Vision for Making Disciples 5

Exercise #1 11

#1 – A Hearing Heart 13

Exercise #2 17

#2 – Two Elements of Discipleship 19

Handout: Dying to Self 23

Exercise #3 25

#3 – The Nature of the Father 27

Handout: The Father Heart of God 31

Exercise #4 35

#4 – The Nature of the Son 37

Handout: Parable on Life and The Winner's Creed 40

Exercise #5 41

#5 – The Nature of the Holy Spirit 43

Exercise #6 47

#6 - The Traits of a Disciple 49

Exercise #7 53

#7 – A Mature Son of God 55

Exercise #8 61

#8 – A Royal Priest unto God 63

Exercise #9 67

#9 – A Disciple's First Love 69

Conclusion 73

Evaluation 74

Bibliography 75

FOREWORD

This discipleship manual, *Go and Make Disciples!*, provides a way to rekindle the biblical flame for making disciples for the purpose of spiritual maturity and leadership training. These sessions capture the principles that Jesus, the Master disciple-maker, used in building godly character into His men and preparing them for their world-changing ministries. You will find in this book a concentrated, practical approach that imparts a deep spiritual understanding of Jesus' priority in the training of disciples.

Every living species must somehow reproduce in order to survive. Any successful army must produce trained soldiers. A manufacturer must create finished products in order to stay in business. In the same way, the Church (Body of Messiah) must produce disciplined and sanctified lives for it to grow and reproduce in a healthy way.

Having a vision for making disciples means understanding and appreciating the Lord's purposes in spending most of His ministry time with just twelve men. These disciples of Jesus received the full explanation of His teachings and the benefit of personal friendship with Him. When we see that this is still the heart of the Lord's ministry to men and women through the Holy Spirit, we will be willing to invest in others as Jesus did. We need to see that it is normal for a believer to intentionally make disciples since Jesus modeled it, commanded it, and trained His men to do so.

God chose disciple-making as His ultimate means of winning the entire world. However, most believers are made into disciples as a by-product of general church ministry; they have not had someone to personally invest in them. If there is a shortcut to maturity in the kingdom of God, it is when seasoned, mature, godly believers purposefully impart the Word of God to teachable men and women who want to grow in the Lord.

We have found that the best way to use the material in this book is in small groups (four or five persons per group). Within a small group of people of the same gender, there is an easy dynamic of open sharing, accountability, and honest prayer. Most groups meet weekly for a few hours. The written homework is discussed together, and the memory work is shared alongside the homework or interspersed throughout the teaching time. Memorizing Scripture is strongly encouraged, as each memorized verse becomes a tool in the disciple's hand to overcome the enemy and to use in ministering to others.

Since the leader will be giving the teaching, we have found it best for him or her to merely facilitate the exercise-sharing time without sharing a lot personally. As he teaches later, he can enhance the material with personal testimonies or insights related to the subject being covered.

Although we allow one absence for the ten-week series, we strongly encourage everyone to make every class. We emphasize commitment to the Lord, to one's own spiritual growth, and to those in the group for accountability and confidentiality. Building relationship and trust within the group is a big part of the discipleship process. When someone misses a class, he not only misses the teaching, he also misses the group interaction time. As a result, to some degree the camaraderie and unity are adversely affected.

May these sessions open new doors for you in the great adventure of following Jesus and in the enterprise of making disciples!

GETTING ACQUAINTED

When you are beginning a new discipleship group, it is a good idea to have some initial introduction questions for each one in the group to answer. These should be answered briefly, and if the facilitator begins with his (or her) own introduction, it will set the time limit for the others to follow. You may use these or others that are more appropriate to your group.

(1) Where did you grow up? Do you have a family? Tell us a little about yourself.

(2) When did you make a personal, life commitment to Jesus as Messiah and Lord?

What were the circumstances of your spiritual rebirth?

(3) What are you doing with your life now?

The Purpose for a Vision for Discipleship

"And He went up on the mountain and called to Him those He Himself wanted. And they came to Him. Then He appointed twelve that they might be with Him, and that He might send them out to preach, and to have power to heal sicknesses and to cast out demons" (**Mark 3:13-15**).

Jesus called twelve men to be with Him in close relationship. He trained them and then sent them out to do the work of the ministry. In our modern era, intentionally discipling others as Jesus did has been largely neglected. Although most believers will share the gospel with people or perhaps bring them to worship services, very few will actually teach them how to live as a faithful disciple of Jesus. Today's statistics show that the great majority of new believers fall away from the faith. How important it is for us to make personal investments into the lives of others as Jesus did! After introducing them to Jesus in personal relationship, we need to teach them His ways. Not only should they hear His Word through us, they should also see it lived out in our lives.

Just as Jesus had a strategy for making disciples, so should we. The VISION FOR DISCIPLESHIP is aimed at motivating people who are fairly established and mature in the Lord to reach out to others and disciple them. Although this book is not really for new believers, it can be adapted for them. The purpose of this material is to encourage believers to move from complacency and laziness to embrace their call and commission to be a disciple and to make disciples (Matthew 28:19-20). The VISION FOR DISCIPLESHIP will also give believers a format to follow in ongoing discipleship ministry.

In this material we will look closely at the three commissions of our Lord, and we will answer four questions:

• What is a disciple?

• What are the traits of a disciple?

• What does it mean to make disciples?

• What are God's purposes for discipleship?

We hope and pray that you will be among those who disciple others in every place God plants or sends you. Our goal is to see believers everywhere discipled and mature in their walk with God. We believe the Lord desires to have an equipped army ready to reap the harvest and conserve it as He again sends revival throughout the world. And in the face of persecution, it is disciplined believers who will remain faithful and endure to the end. Therefore, it is expedient that people not only find Jesus as their Messiah, but also that they yield to His lordship and grow into His likeness as His disciple.

Our Master's last words should be our first priority, *"Go into all the world and preach the gospel to every creature"* (**Mark 16:15**), and *"Go and make disciples of all the nations…"* (**Matt. 28:19**).

A VISION FOR MAKING DISCIPLES

"And Jesus came and spoke to them, saying, 'All authority has been given to Me in heaven and on earth. Go therefore and make disciples of all the nations, baptizing them in the name of the Father and of the Son and of the Holy Spirit, teaching them to observe all things that I have commanded you; and lo, I am with you always, even to the end of the age.' Amen." (**Matt. 28:18-20**).

A disciple or a follower?

A disciple is a person who humbles himself to be taught by another. Eager to please his teacher, he embraces disciplines and makes lifestyle changes. A disciple of Jesus is committed to obeying and serving Him. He wants to live for the Father's pleasure and be a blessing to Him and others. Many people believe in Jesus but do not really follow Him. A follower has his own interests in mind. He may appreciate the salvation Jesus offers, but he chooses to live for his own pleasure and gain. Rather than desiring to be a blessing, he follows Jesus for the blessings he can receive.

Being a disciple is being willing to leave everything to follow the Master wherever He leads. It is choosing to obey all that He says. True discipleship is a full commitment to His Lordship. As far as the Bible is concerned, there is no Christianity apart from discipleship. Christianity is defined biblically in terms of its maximum expression, not its minimum requirements.

Proverbs 29:18 says, *"Where there is no revelation* [prophetic vision]*, the people cast off restraint; but happy is he who keeps the law."* The Hebrew text for this verse is rich. It says that when people do not perceive God's vision for their lives, they are aimless and without direction; they run in circles until they disintegrate. But if they have vision for keeping His law and obeying His commandments, they will be blessed.

God wants to give us vision for making disciples! Unless we understand that we are called to make disciples, we will fail to get alongside new or struggling believers to help them mature in the Lord. Instead, we will leave them to see to their own spiritual growth. Many believers never reach maturity in Jesus because they have not been properly discipled by more mature believers. We need to realize that we ARE our "brothers' keepers" (Gen. 4:9-10), and take our responsibility seriously before God to care for the spiritual welfare of others. To disciple someone in the faith is to be personally involved in his or her life for the purpose of intentional spiritual development.

The ministry style of Jesus

Jesus had a very effective ministry style. He preached to thousands of followers, taught hundreds in synagogues, trained at least seventy disciples, and chose twelve disciples for closer friendship and additional training. From the twelve men, Jesus chose three as special friends to mentor further. Let us look at this in more detail.

Jesus preached the gospel to the multitudes (thousands), taught them about the kingdom of God, healed their sick, and delivered them from demonic oppression. He not only cared for their spiritual needs, He also met some of their physical needs. On two occasions He multiplied food to give them. Jesus felt a great responsibility to the multitudes (*see* Matt. 4:23-25; 14:14-21, Luke 5:15).

He described His ministry to the people in **Luke 4:18-19**: *"The Spirit of the Lord is upon Me, because He has anointed Me to preach the gospel to the poor; He has sent Me to heal the brokenhearted, to proclaim liberty to the captives, and recovery of sight to the blind, to set at liberty those who are oppressed; to proclaim the acceptable year of the Lord."*

Jesus also preached and taught in synagogues on the Sabbath to hundreds of people. He often healed people of physical infirmities while in their synagogues (*see* Matt. 4:23; Luke 4:15-16, 31, 44).

Jesus discipled at least 70 people who followed Him closely. These He trained to preach, heal, and cast out demons. He sent them out ahead of Himself to villages and cities (Luke 10:1-3). The Lord also selected a smaller group of men to strategically teach and train as future apostles. These are the 12 disciples who were with Him almost all the time from when He called them. Most of them (if not all) spent about three years living alongside Jesus. They were appointed by the Lord to be with Him in order to learn from Him. Then they were to go out in His power to extend His work (Mark 3:13-15, Matt. 28:16-20).

Jesus' ministry to His disciples

John 17:6a, 8 describes Jesus' ministry to His twelve disciples: *"I have manifested Your name to the men whom You have given Me out of the world... I have given to them the words which You have given Me; and they have received them, and have known surely that I came forth from You; and they have believed that You sent Me."* Of these twelve, Jesus chose three men—Peter, James and John—who would be His closer companions. These He mentored into leadership. They were with Him at special times when the others were not (*see* Matt. 26:37-38; 17:1).

Jesus revealed God's name (His Person, nature, and character) to His disciples. He recognized that the men following Him belonged to God, so He taught them with care and respect. Jesus did not try to disciple everyone. He only trained those whom the Father gave Him; into them He poured His life, wisdom, and knowledge. He showed them through example how to disciple others, and then, with authority, He sent them out to do so. **John 17:18** says, *"As You sent Me out into the world, I also have sent them out into the world."*

Jesus sent His disciples out to:
 + preach the gospel and heal the sick
 + reveal the character and love of the Father
 + convince others of the divinity of Jesus
 + disciple people in their personal relationships with God and the Scriptures.

Our calling as the Lord's present-day disciples is the same as that of Jesus and His original men: (1) We are to minister to the multitudes in the power of the Spirit through preaching, teaching and healing. (2) We are to disciple others in their relationship with the Lord. (3) If we are spiritual leaders, we should be able to discern and recognize God's call on individuals for leadership and spend time training and mentoring them.

One of the dangers of being busy in ministry is that we can end up loving crowds but not really caring for individuals. Or wanting contributors, but not wanting to spend time meeting people's individual needs. Years ago a man decided to visit the churches of two well-known television ministers he liked. After hearing the first, he asked if he could say hello to him. But the minister's bodyguards said no, suggesting he phone to arrange an appointment.

Disappointed, he went to hear the other minister, and was invited to lunch with him following the service. Feeling valued, he handed the minister a check for four million dollars. (This is a true story.) We must always be approachable, available, and affirming. We cannot personally minister to all who are sick and counsel all who are hurting. But Jesus was *"...touched with the feeling of our infirmities..."* (**Heb. 4:15 KJV**) as He mingled with people. Only as we stay in touch with the needs of people, can God use us to meet those needs.

Three commissions to obey

The commissions regarding the souls of men that Jesus gave to His disciples should be of top priority within the life of every believer. We will consider the main three: to pray for laborers for the harvest, to preach the gospel, and to produce disciples.

The first commission is found in **Matthew 9:37-38**: *"Then He said to His disciples, 'The harvest truly is plentiful, but the workers are few. Therefore pray to the Lord of the harvest to send out laborers into His harvest.'"* We have a mandate from God to pray for workers for His harvest. This should be a regular part of our prayer lives! People all over the world are dying without knowledge of God's salvation in Jesus. We must petition the Father to send workers into His harvest fields!

Usually, the more we pray for laborers, the more we want to be among those that go! The opposite is also true: the less we pray for workers to be sent into the harvest fields, the more we will feel comfortable staying where we are. The late Keith Green wrote a song with these words: *"The Lord commands us to go; why do so many feel called to stay?"*

Jesus gave us a second commission in **Mark 16:15**: *"And He said to them, 'Go into all the world and preach the gospel to every creature.'"* We are to share with everyone the good news of salvation made possible through the death and resurrection of Jesus Christ. Our ministry should include praying for the sick and casting out demons, according to Mark 16:17-18. *"...my speech and my preaching were not with persuasive words of human wisdom, but in demonstration of the spirit and power, that your faith should not be in the wisdom of men but in the power of God"* (**1 Cor. 2:4-5**).

A third commission, commonly called the Great Commission, is found in **Matthew 28:18-20**: *"Go therefore and make disciples of all the nations, baptizing them in the name of the Father and of the Son and of the Holy Spirit, teaching them to observe all things that I have commanded you; and lo, I am with you always, even to the end of the age."* We are commissioned to make disciples. Intentional, strategic disciple making is the surest way to bring new believers into a mature understanding of the Lord and His ways. To make a disciple requires us to teach, mentor, and model the lifestyle of Jesus. It is not just the informing of facts; it is imparting His life.

Multiplication principle of disciple making

To illustrate how important and powerful strategic discipling is, imagine an evangelist who could win 1,000 souls to Jesus every day for 80 years. In that amount of time, he would win 29,200,000 souls. What a tremendous accomplishment! But, consider this: if one person faithfully disciples another person for a year and then those two disciple one person each the next year… If those four faithfully disciple one person each for a year, and the resulting eight people disciple eight more the next year, and so on… In 33 years of faithful disciple-making, 8,589,934,592 would be discipled!

The attack against making disciples

One of the greatest attacks against the Body of Christ is in the area of intentional disciple making. Throughout history, the Body of Christ has been its weakest when the ministry of making disciples has been lost, neglected, or forgotten. Today, over 2000 years since the redemption plan was initiated, the world is not yet won to Jesus because most believers are not actively making disciples. The Church has been debilitated because countless believers have not been trained how to study God's Word and apply His principles to their lives. Many have distorted perceptions of God and faulty doctrines because they have had no one to invest in them personally. They have not been taught how to grow in their knowledge of the Lord. Rather than reaching spiritual maturity and discipling others, they have remained spiritually immature (Heb. 5:12-14). Dr. Keith Phillips says, *"Discipleship is the only way to produce both the quantity and quality of believers God desires."*

Spiritual leaders have failed by not investing time and energy to disciple believers and equip them to share the load of ministry. Leaders are busy in many areas of service, but they often neglect this crucial work of making disciples. If only they could see that the Lord's ordained method for building His Body and preparing ministries was and still is personal disciple making!

Lasting fruit

We are commissioned not to make converts, but to make disciples. Unfortunately, we have many "infant deaths" within God's kingdom. Recent statistics show that 80-90% of new believers fall away from the faith within the first year of committing themselves to Jesus. God does not want us to just bear fruit; He wants us to bear fruit that remains! In **John 15:16** Jesus said, *"You have not chosen Me, but I chose you and appointed you that you should go and bear fruit, and that your fruit should remain, that whatever you ask the Father in My name He may give you."* Strategic discipling is one of the ways we can bear lasting fruit.

In *My Utmost for His Highest*, devotional writer Oswald Chambers wrote:

Our work begins where God's grace has laid the foundation; we are not to save souls, but to disciple them. Salvation and sanctification are the work of God's sovereign grace; our work as His disciples is to disciple lives until they are completely yielded and surrendered to God. One life wholly yielded to God is of more value to God than 100 lives simply awakened by His Spirit. God brings us to a standard of life by His grace, and we are responsible for reproducing that standard in others.

Pastor Rick Joyner expressed these prophetic words in his book, *The Harvest Volume 2*:

"When revival has come in the past, the Body of Christ has seldom been prepared for it. This time can be different. The Lord is moving on mature, stable men and women of God to prepare to raise these new spiritual infants so they will not be lost again to the world. Newborn believers are dependent on the Body to provide for them spiritually until they are mature enough to take care of themselves. Now is the time for us to all prepare by sinking our own roots deeper into the Word of God and by developing our personal relationships with Him. We must know what we believe and know how to teach it. Let us prepare now before the flood comes.

First, we must get our own lives in order, eliminating any sin or compromise. These are the King's own children He is entrusting us to teach. Let us not only be careful how we teach them, but how we live. Our lives will be teaching them just as much as the knowledge we impart. The Lord said that after one has been taught he "becomes like his teacher."

American disciple maker, Stephen Vogel, penned these thoughts:

We need discipleship so that…

- we can grow up into spiritual maturity and into the likeness of Jesus.
- new believers can have their questions answered.
- all believers can be ready and able to give a defense of the hope that is within them.
- every believer can be equipped to lead a lost soul to Christ.
- parents can teach their children the Word of God with confidence and wisdom.
- children can observe the Lord's character and conduct lived out in their homes.
- parents can teach their children how to pray effectively.
- believers struggling with sin will have someone with whom to be accountable.
- believers will be doers of the Word and not simply hearers.
- people will know how to search the Scriptures for themselves.
- believers will know how to put their faith into action.
- the Body of Christ can be built up by each member.
- we will stand strong in faith while enduring trials or persecution.

• Pause for some time and pray that the Lord will send laborers into His harvest fields.

• Pray for His salvation to be released to your family members, friends, city, and nation.

• Ask the Lord into whom you should be investing your life and the Word of God.

Begin to pray that that God will give you His vision regarding the ministry of disciple-making and how you can best fulfill this Great Commission.

EXERCISE #1 – A HEARING HEART

Please Memorize:

Isaiah 50:4-5 – *"The Lord God has given Me the tongue of disciples, that I may know how to sustain the weary one with a word. He awakens Me morning by morning; He awakens My ear to listen as a disciple. The Lord God has opened my ear, and I was not rebellious, nor did I turn away."* (NASB)

Luke 6:40 – *"A disciple is not above his teacher, but everyone who is fully trained will be like his teacher."*

---

* Pray <u>every day</u> this week for God to give you a vision for making disciples.

1. What are the three commissions that every disciple of Jesus should obey? (Matt. 9:37-38, Mark 16:15; 28:18-20)

2. Have you been personally discipled? Explain.

3. Have you ever discipled someone? If so, what method or program did you use?

4. List some qualities that you believe should be present in one who disciples another.

5. How would you describe a disciple of Jesus Christ?

6. What would you suggest to someone who wants to grow in his or her knowledge of the Lord?

7. According to Isaiah 50:4-5, what is one of the distinguishing marks of a disciple?

8. Read Jeremiah 11:1-17. Why was God angry with His people?

9. How do you hear God best?

Do you have a set appointment time for the Lord daily? If so, when?

10. Read Matthew 4:19-22. What did the men leave behind when Jesus called them?

Can you relate to this? If so, how?

Is there something you are clinging to that God wants you to leave behind?

#1 – A HEARING HEART

A disciple is one who leaves everything in order to follow Jesus. Because he has a strong desire to learn and change, he is always seeking further instruction, transformation, and equipping. A disciple is so teachable that he can hear God's wisdom even through a person he may naturally dislike or disrespect. Those who long to hear God's voice will be listening for Him through anyone.

Read Isaiah 50:4-5 (NASB). As the Lord's disciples, we are to listen for His words every day—not only for our own lives, but also for the purpose of encouraging others.

Listening for God's voice

In **Luke 8:18** Jesus said, *"Take heed how you hear. For whoever has, to him more will be given; and whoever does not have, even what he seems to have will be taken from him."* The ability to hear and recognize God's voice increases as we attentively listen to Him. If we do not listen carefully, we will gradually lose our sensitivity to the Lord's voice. We need to train our ears, and cultivate our ability to hear.

Isaiah 55:3a says, *"Incline your ear, and come to Me. Hear, and your soul shall live."* This verse speaks of actively listening to God. We must choose to listen to Him and take steps toward Him. Hearing God's voice leads to intimacy with Him. Intimacy with Him leads to passionate love for Him and zeal in serving Him.

"Be still [cease striving; stop] *and know that I am God"* (**Ps. 46:10**). We must make time to be still and silent! When we are quiet, we can more easily hear the voice of our Master. There is a discipline of silence and solitude that many in the Body of Christ are missing today. Our busy lives tend to crowd out stillness and silence. As a result, we are not hearing the Lord speak as we should. We are forfeiting His counsel to us and are failing to cultivate our love relationship with Him.

Sometimes we try to make every moment count. While we eat, we read the Bible or listen to a CD. When we walk or drive, we pray or sing aloud. We are seldom silent. We must understand that if God is to speak in a quiet voice to our spirits, we need some times of silence to be able to hear Him! We have to discipline our minds and our mouths to be still. If we do, we will enter into a whole new dimension of rest in Him. We will more clearly distinguish His voice from other voices. Our relationship with Jesus will deepen, and our security and confidence in Him will grow. Learning to listen is a vital discipline that each of us must cultivate!

Job 13:5 says, *"Oh, that you would be quiet and it should be to your wisdom."* It is silence which guards and feeds the fire and zeal of God within us. Silence ignites passion for His will and His glory. The men of spiritual passion in the Scriptures (such as Moses, King David, and Jesus) all knew the value of solitude. They had times of quiet, intimate communion with the Father, knowing that to hear His heart demanded a time of intimacy in stillness. We can hear spoken commands from a distance, but we have to be very close to someone to hear his heart.

God considers the aspect of listening to be of primary importance! Most of the Old Testament prophets were in anguish concerning the refusal of Israel to hear God's voice. They urged them to repent. Those in spiritual leadership were especially confronted! God expects more from those who are serving His people. Leaders must listen! *"And from everyone who has been given much shall much be required"* (**Luke 12:48**).

Read Psalm 81:8-13. God cries out for us to listen to Him! He urges us to sit in His presence and listen to His counsel. The noise of self-interests, distractions, activities, and cares can muffle the Father's voice and instruction, so we must make time to hear Him. We need to set aside time where we give the Lord our undivided attention.

God's process for spiritual growth

(1) He speaks – through the Scriptures and to our spirits directly, through preaching and teaching, and through others.

(2) I listen – We must choose to listen to Him and be willing to obey.

(3) I believe – We hear what He says, and by a choice of our will, we believe it.

(4) I apply – We receive the Word humbly and are *"doers of the Word, and not hearers only"* (**Jam. 1:22**).

(5) I am changed – As we apply God's instructions to our lives, we are changed.

If we struggle with the sin of unbelief, we hear the Word but we refuse to believe it is true for us. Instead, we believe what we see or have experienced in the past although it is in sharp contrast to God's plans for us. If we refuse to believe God's Word by faith we will not apply it and embrace change. We must repent of all unbelief and renounce it as sin!

If we are guilty of pride, we refuse to receive correction. We may see the truth but we do not think we have to apply it like others do. We believe that God has a shortcut for us! We may think, "Everyone else needs to serve, but I am not called to… It is good for Christians to give, but I do not have to." Unbelief causes us to believe that we are below the law of grace, and that what is available to others concerning God's provision is not available to us. Pride causes us to believe we are above the law and that what applies to others does not apply to us.

If we follow the above steps correctly, we will cultivate humility and faith (see Rom. 10:17) and intimacy with the Lord. We will become more like Jesus.

Hearing and overcoming are linked

To all seven churches in Revelation 2-3, Jesus says two common things: (1) *"He that has an ear to hear, let him hear what the Spirit says to the churches."* and (2) *"He that overcomes shall I give…"*

There is a strong link between hearing and overcoming! It is possible that our ability to overcome the world, the flesh, and the devil are in direct proportion to our hearing the voice of the Holy Spirit.

In **John 10:27** Jesus said, *"My sheep* (the mature ones—sheep, not lambs) *hear My voice, and I know them, and they follow Me."* A disciple is one who has trained his spiritual ears to recognize the voice of his Master. He is actively listening for His voice and ready to obey His instructions. He delights to do the Father's will.

The cost of discipleship

Notice what Jesus' first disciples did in Matthew 4:20-22:

(1) The men immediately left their nets and boat, which represented their vocations, identity, and financial security. They left what was comfortable and familiar to them. To follow Jesus as His disciple means we are committed to Him, even if we have to leave our securities, identities, and comforts. We trust God to supply all our needs. Whether He does that through employment or supernatural provision, we recognize that He is our source of supply (*see* Phil. 4:19).

(2) The men left their father. This shows the cost of discipleship in view of close relationships (*see* Luke 14:26-27, Ps. 45:10-11). We are to love and cherish the Lord above all others.

(3) They left what they had envisioned for their futures and followed Jesus without reservation. A true disciple has no reservation in following the Master.

The Lord calls us out of our former ways of living to follow Him, belong to Him, and be a part of establishing His kingdom on earth and in the lives of others. This may require us to make difficult decisions regarding relationships and employment, but anything we have to give up for the Lord's sake is worth it. We give up everything, but we gain everything that matters!

EXERCISE #2 – TWO ELEMENTS OF DISCIPLESHIP

> **Please Memorize:**
>
> **Matthew 28:18-20** – *"And Jesus came and spoke to them saying, 'All authority has been given to Me in heaven and on earth. Go therefore and make disciples of all the nations, baptizing them in the name of the Father and of the Son and of the Holy Spirit, teaching them to observe all things that I have commanded you; and lo, I am with you always, even to the end of the age. Amen.'"*

* Pray for a vision for making disciples and for those in your discipleship or small group.

1. Write out the words of Jesus to His disciples found in Matthew 28:18-20, adding the word "you" before every command.

2. In reference to the power and authority of Jesus, read Colossians 1:16-18 and Ephesians 1:19-22. Notice and list how often the word 'all' is used.

3. The apostle Paul taught by example. Read 1 Corinthians 11:1-2; 4:16, and Philippians 3:17; 4:9. Who is observing and following your example?

4. What are the central elements of discipleship that we see in Romans 8:29, Matthew 28:19-20, and 2 Timothy 2:2?

5. According to 1 Corinthians 1:18, where is the power of God found for those who believe in Jesus?

6. Read James 3:16. What by-products of self-seeking do you see?

Pause and reflect on your life. Do you see the truth of this when you demand your own way?

7. Read 1 John 3:16-18. When we really grasp God's love for us, what will be our response?

List some ways we can obey these verses practically.

8. Read Romans 6:1-11 and Hebrews 9:26-28. How would you explain to someone how we "die with Jesus" and how we "live with Him?"

9. Why did John the Baptist say, *"He must increase, but I must decrease"*?

What is the purpose behind our decreasing after He increases in us, and not vice-versa? (Should we not decrease first so that there is room in us for Him to increase?)

10. Read and meditate on 2 Timothy 3:1-5, asking the Lord to show you any areas of sin that you need to confess and renounce.

#2 – Two Elements of Discipleship

"And Jesus came and spoke to them, saying, 'All authority has been given to Me in heaven and on earth'" (**Matt. 28:18**). *"He [Jesus] is the image of the invisible God, the firstborn over all creation. For by Him all things were created that are in heaven and that are on earth, visible and invisible, whether thrones or dominions or principalities or powers. All things were created through Him and for Him. And He is before all things, and in Him all things consist. And He is the head of the body, the church, who is the beginning, the firstborn from the dead, that in all things He may have the preeminence"* (**Col. 1:15-18**).

Jesus, as God and co-creator of all, with unlimited power, has every right to command us to bring everyone to a place of submitting fully under His Lordship and authority. *"Go therefore and make disciples of all the nations, baptizing them in the name of the Father and the Son and the Holy Spirit, teaching them to observe all things that I have commanded you..."* (**Matt. 28:19-20a**).

Three-fold command in making disciples

Jesus said if we will bring others into a yielded, disciplined relationship with Him, He will always be with us (*see* Matt. 28:20b). He gave us a three-fold command in making disciples: (1) reach all people with the gospel, (2) baptize them into His name, and (3) teach them His commands. Let's look at Jesus' command in more detail.

(1) *"...make disciples of all nations [ethnic groups]."* As disciples of Jesus, we are commissioned to disciple others until they submit to Him. All people in every nation need to be discipled! In addition to reaching unbelievers for the Lord and discipling them in the faith and in God's Word, we are to disciple those who already believe but are not yet mature in their walk with Him. Every believer must be discipled!

(2) *"Baptizing them in the name of the Father, the Son and the Holy Spirit."* In the Greek language, the word **baptizo** means, "to make fully wet." Water baptism is an important act of obedience whereby the power of our sinful nature is cut off. It is the outward symbol that we have experienced the death and burial of our old nature through the remission of our sin, and that we are resurrected to a new life in Christ Jesus. All believers in Jesus are to undergo water baptism (Mark 16:16, Acts 2:28). It is the sign of the circumcision of the heart in the New Covenant.

To be baptized into the name of the Father, Son, and Holy Spirit is more than just the act of water baptism. The Greek word for 'name' is **onoma**, which implies character, rank, authority, or nature. Our task is to baptize those who believe in Jesus into a knowledge and experience of the three-fold nature of the Godhead. To do that, we must know God as Father, know Jesus as His Son, and know the Person and ministry of the Holy Spirit.

When we begin to disciple others, we first introduce them to God as Father. There is much to know about God, but Jesus stressed that we must know Him as Father! We are invited to have a close, loving relationship with Him. God revealed part of His nature to Moses in Exodus 34:5-7, where we read that He is merciful, gracious, patient, and good. In other Scriptures, we read that God is righteous, just, and holy. He is slow to get angry and loves unconditionally. He is worthy of our love, worship, and respect. As disciples, we also need to allow the Father to live through us in compassion, truth, goodness, and righteousness. We are to love unconditionally and be slow to anger. We must know Him, teach about Him, and impart His life to others.

Second, we are to immerse people into the knowledge and experience of Jesus as Son. As a son, Jesus was obedient, humble, a servant, and faithful in prayer. He only did what He saw the Father do, and only said what the Father told Him to say. He was compassionate and wise. He knew the Scriptures. We need to know Him personally, and be able to show Him to others through how we live. We, as God's sons, are to be humble servants, prayerful, gentle and loving, and students of God's Word.

Third, we are to bring people into the knowledge of and experience of the Person of the Holy Spirit. He is the Spirit of Truth, the Helper, Counselor, Comforter, Strengthener, and Intercessor. He reminds us of Jesus' words. He empowers us to minister as Jesus did, and sustains us through trials. He reveals the Father's heart and will to us to help us pray effectively. We need to know these truths about the Holy Spirit through experience, not just through head knowledge, and we must be able to teach them to others. When the Holy Spirit is living through us, we are able to help, comfort, and counsel. We get alongside people and strengthen them in their struggles. We intercede!

(3) *"Teaching them to observe all that I have commanded you."* After we establish people in their relationship with the Lord, we teach them to obey His commands. As the Lord's representatives, we model His life, teach His commands, and mentor believers in serving Him. Those we disciple should be able to observe the Lord's commands lived out in our lives.

Transformation into the likeness of Jesus

The first element of discipleship is transformation into the image of Jesus through dying to self and living to God (Galatians 2:20). We must embrace the culture of God's Kingdom and turn from our carnal ways that are in opposition to God's will.

The world today is self-centered, proud, ungrateful, angry, and violent. It loves pleasure and mocks true righteousness and godliness. Although many people are religious to a degree, they deny the power of God because they have not embraced the cross of Jesus. Too often this is also true of believers. In contrast to our carnal self-absorption, we serve a God Who did not protect Himself in self-love. He poured out His life to the point of death for the eternal salvation of others. True love is always a pouring out of oneself for the sake of another; it is to give all that we have and are that others might live and be blessed. The Apostle Paul's chief goal in life was to be transformed into everything that Jesus is. Notice what he wrote in Philippians 3:12-14.

In **John 13:34** Jesus said, *"... love one another as I have loved you."* Jesus commands us to lay down our lives for others, to say "no" to selfishness for the good of someone else. Our maturity in Jesus shows when we, in our love for God and others, deny our own wishes and rights for their sake. At every age and in all circumstances, we are to deny ourselves and prefer others. Love of self comes naturally to all of us, but once we are born again, our love for God should have center stage in our hearts and lives. As we abide in Jesus and walk in the power of the Holy Spirit, we can love others as God has loved us.

To trust in Jesus is to commit ourselves to Him, giving Him complete access to our lives. To be 'in Christ' means there is an exchange and interchange of His character with ours. That is what being born-again is all about! It is the only way a self-centered, self-serving individual can ever be changed into a selfless, self-giving child of God. Only Jesus can give us rest from the bondage of self-love and its destructive consequences, such as selfishness, strife, and damaged relationships.

Practical ways we can prefer others

— Listening respectfully when another is talking, without interrupting or planning a response.

— Serving where possible; being accessible to others; giving up our privacy.

— Honoring those in authority: government leaders, pastors, parents, and husbands.

— Denying our fleshly appetites if indulging them will offend someone.

— Taking the smallest portion or the broken cookie. Putting others first.

— Sacrificing our time or desires to help another.

— Forgiving those who hurt or humiliate us.

Reproducing Jesus' character into the lives of disciples

The second element of discipleship is reproducing the life and character of Jesus into others. It is bringing people to salvation in Jesus and then teaching them how to study God's Word and apply it to their lives. It is teaching them to be disciplined in prayer and in hearing God's voice. All that God has invested into us regarding His kingdom is to be invested into others. It is not only a privilege to receive the faith, it is also our duty to give it away! We are the links between God and those who have yet to know Him as we do.

"You therefore, my son, be strong in the grace that is in Christ Jesus. And the things that you have heard from me among many witnesses, commit these to faithful men who will be able to teach others also" (**2 Tim. 2:1-2**). The Greek word translated "faithful" is **pistos**, which means 'believing, loyal, and reliable.' Choose people who are reliable and dependable when you are looking for people to disciple. Look for those who are teachable and have servants' hearts.

Jesus was disciplined in the principles of the kingdom of God, and He imparted those disciplines to His men. The Apostle Paul did the same. He received His Father's vision of making disciples and passed it on, sharing it with Timothy and others. Now it is our generation and our turn. One of the highest honors and responsibilities with which we can be entrusted is to care for new believers by spiritually feeding and tending them.

Someone once said, *"Too many Christians today are like mules: hard workers with strong opinions and convictions, but unable to reproduce."* We need to be able to reproduce the Lord's character, conduct, and ministry strategy into others through teaching and modeling it. But before we can disciple anyone, we must be disciples ourselves; only then is there an anointing to transfer spiritual disciplines to others. Those you disciple will develop your level of discipline. Do you want people to pray? Then be faithful as an intercessor. Do you want them to love the Bible? Love it, read it, and study it faithfully. Your strengths and weaknesses will be imparted to those you disciple.

Our gospel is flawed if it does not accurately present the cross. We must teach the importance of denying ourselves and embracing the Lordship of Jesus. Our discipleship is flawed if we do not lead believers through the cross to a personal love relationship with Jesus. Ultimately, it is our love for and commitment to Him that motivate us to pursue personal holiness. That same motivation should inspire us to bring others into a disciplined, love relationship with Him.

DYING TO SELF

When you are forgotten or neglected, and you do not hurt with the insult or the oversight, but instead your heart is happy, being counted worthy to suffer for Jesus—that is DYING TO SELF.

When your good is misunderstood and criticized, your advice disregarded, and your opinions ridiculed, and you refuse to defend yourself or let anger rise in your heart, embracing it all in patient silence—that is DYING TO SELF.

When you lovingly and patiently bear any disorder, any irregularity, any impunctuality or any annoyance; when you can stand face to face with waste, folly, extravagance, or spiritual insensitivity... and endure it as Jesus endured it—that is DYING TO SELF.

When you are content with any food, any clothing, any climate, any society, any solitude, and any interruption by the will of God—that is DYING TO SELF.

When you never care to refer to yourself in conversation, to record your own good works, or to desire commendation; when you can truly love to be unknown—that is DYING TO SELF.

When you can see your brother prosper and have his needs met, and can honestly rejoice with him in spirit and feel no envy nor question God, while your own needs are far greater and in desperate circumstances—that is DYING TO SELF.

When you can receive correction and reproof from one of less stature than yourself, and can humbly submit inwardly as well as outwardly, finding no rebellion or resentment rising up within your heart—that is DYING TO SELF.

Are you dead yet?

It is the desire of the Holy Spirit to bring each one of us to the cross of Jesus.

"... that I may know Him... being made conformable to His death" (**Phil. 3:10**)

EXERCISE #3 – THE NATURE OF THE FATHER

* Pray for a vision for making disciples and for those in your discipleship group.

1. Read Psalm 103 and make a list of God's attributes (excellent qualities) mentioned there.

2. How is God described in Deuteronomy 32:4?

3. Read John 14:6-16 and notice everything Jesus says about the Father. List your observations.

4. One of the chief tactics of the enemy is to distort God's character so that you will walk in fear and unbelief rather than in faith and love. From the following verses, what aspects of God's Fatherhood toward you do you see?

Jeremiah 31:3

_____

Romans 8:38-39

_____

Ephesians 1:4-6

_____

Galatians 4:4-6

_____

Isaiah 46:3-4

_____

Isaiah 43:4

_____

Psalm 23:1-2

_____

Hebrews 13:5

_____

Matthew 28:20

_____

John 10:27-29

_____

Hebrews 12:6-11

_____

5. Think about your earthly father for a few minutes. How would you compare him with your heavenly Father? In what ways is he like Him or unlike Him?

6. Read Psalm 27:10. What does this mean to you? Have you experienced this truth personally?

7. What aspect of God's Fatherhood is most real to you? Why?

#3 – THE NATURE OF THE FATHER

Begin this session by quoting Matthew 28:18-20 together in your small group… To look at what it means to be baptized into the name [nature, character] of God as Father, we will begin by considering some truths from the Scriptures about the overall character of God: God has infinite wisdom, power, and knowledge. He is eternal (He always has been and always will be). He is everywhere all the time and full of glory. The Bible says many things about God's attributes; there are two we want to especially point out:

(1) God is love. He loves unselfishly and unconditionally. His love never ends. *"He who does not love does not know God, for God is love"* (**1 John 4:8**).

(2) God is holy. He is always righteous and just. **1 Peter 1:16** says, *"It is written, 'Be holy for I am holy.' "* **Revelation 4:8b** says, *"Holy, holy, holy, Lord God Almighty, Who was and Who is and Who is to come!"*

God demonstrated both His holiness and His love by sending His sinless Son, Jesus, to die as a sacrifice for our sins. In His holiness, He cannot overlook sin, and in His love, He could not help but make a plan for man's salvation. *"God demonstrates His own love toward us, in that while we were yet sinners, Christ died for us"* (**Rom. 5:8**).

God loves everyone unconditionally and eternally, and He will always unselfishly do what is right. However, we do not always perceive Him that way. Our perceptions of God come from a variety of influences, some of which are very different from what the Scriptures reveal about Him.

The power of our perception of God

Our concept of God influences every area of our lives. It determines how we relate to ourselves, to others, and to every situation we encounter. Theologian A.W. Tozer wrote, *"What comes into our minds when we think about God is the most important thing about us."*

Why is it so easy to hold a wrong image of God in our hearts despite the clear teaching of Scripture about Him? Because the negative things we learn and experience in our early relationships with those close to us are so deep and powerful that they reduce the teaching of Scripture to mere head knowledge. Our faulty views of God can cause us to fear intimacy with Him, or inspire to us to labor for Him out of duty or fear rather than out of love. They affect how we worship Him (Are we convinced that He is worthy of our worship?). Our witness will also be affected; the more we admire and adore Him, the more we want others to know and love Him like we do. We can rise no higher in our spiritual life than our view or concept of God. This is a key for us as disciples and disciple makers!

Those who have had healthy relationships with their earthly fathers can usually relate positively to God as Father. Those who have had struggles or disappointments in their primary relationships often find relating to God difficult. Most people who have serious problems relating to God as Father have a painful history with their own fathers.

Our concept of God is filtered through our relationships with significant authority figures from our formative years. It is not uncommon to hear a statement such as this, "I love Jesus, but I can't relate to God. My father abused me." Most of us need some degree of healing in our souls to correct our distortions of God's Fatherhood and to mend the wounds of the past. We need to know and believe in God's unconditional love for us and to allow that love to heal us within. The hurts we bear are usually beyond the healing of human love alone. We need God's love. His love far outweighs the hurts in our inner man; it has the power to free us from emotional pain. Each of us must know this love of God for ourselves. We have all been hurt; we all have a love deficit that only His love can fill.

While needing God's love, we also need to repent of our reactions to our pain—what we have become as a result of the hurts we have received. Often we have become bitter, fearful, angry, and critical. Psalm 41:4 says, "Lord, be merciful to me. Heal my soul, for I have sinned against You." To appreciate God's love we must turn from our iniquities and sin. *"Your iniquities have separated you from your God, and your sins have hidden His face from you"* (**Isa. 59:2**).

Relating to authority figures

As mentioned before, we are inclined to see God the way our authority figures (parents, guardians, grandparents, pastors, teachers) have represented Him to us. Here is how our minds make that connection: as children, we tend to see our guardians as gods. They clothe us, feed us, and meet our needs. We are small; they are big and strong! So when we think of God, we picture them.

As we grow older and begin to relate personally to the Lord, we perceive Him to be like our guardians. We expect to receive from Him the same injustices we received from them. In our minds, we transfer onto God their limitations and personality traits. We perceive God through glasses colored by our guardians' mannerisms instead of seeing our heavenly Father as He really is.

…If our parents were critical or condemning, we see God as harsh, critical, and hard to please.

…If our guardians ridiculed us, we fear trusting God with our true selves, fearful that He will mock us.

…If our parents' love was conditional, we find it difficult to understand and accept God's free grace and unconditional love. We tend to work hard to get His acceptance and approval.

…If they did not have time for us or were not available to us, then we do not see God as caring about the small details of our lives.

…If our parents failed to sympathize with us, then we assume that God will not understand us.

...If our father was weak, passive and dominated by others (especially by his wife), we may perceive God as passive and weak, easily rebelled against and controlled.

...If we grew up fatherless, we often see God as missing, unavailable, and uninterested.

...If we were allowed to have our own way as children, then when God withholds something from us, we believe He does not love us.

Where our parents (guardians) failed us, we expect God to fail us also. In our hearts we judge them as inadequate, and we transfer that judgment onto God. Sometimes we need to separate our concept of God from our experiences with authority figures. Then we must accept that what the Bible says about God is absolutely true—He really is almighty, loving, and wise.

Seeing God in perspective

"And we have known and believed the love that God has for us..." (**1 John 4:16**). We must believe in our hearts that God does love us unconditionally, not just know it in our minds. We must welcome His love deep into our souls where it can heal us and set us free. At the same time, we need to realize the justice of God regarding our sin. He is holy and requires us to be holy. 1 Corinthians 1:30 says that Jesus became for us righteousness, sanctification, and redemption. When we are in Him, He imparts His faith, purity, and holiness to us. Then it is up to us, by His grace, to work out that salvation into our everyday lives.

If we only focus on God's mercy and love, we will cheapen His grace in our lives. And if we only see His judgment of sin, we will fear intimacy with Him. We must perceive the Lord as He really is, with the proper balance of mercy and truth, grace and justice. As we worship God in His holiness, we will find that we become more whole and holy ourselves.

Knowing the Father's love

Jesus' main purpose in coming to earth was to reveal the Father to us and to reconcile us to Him. If we stop at salvation and do not cultivate a relationship with the Father, then we have missed Jesus' ultimate purpose in coming. Relationship with the Father is our destination!

"Children's children are the crown of old men, and the glory of children is their father" (**Prov. 17:6**). In the earthly realm, it is the father that gives his children self-worth and an identity as masculine or feminine. To a great extent, he is responsible for the child's self-image and security. The same is true in the spiritual realm. It is our heavenly Father Who gives us our self-worth and security. He gives us our identity as His children and our self-image through His Word, which tells us we are precious to Him. His love for us proves how He values us!

Parent me!

Even if our parents (guardians) have failed or rejected us, we can feel loved and valued by knowing the love of the Father. We attain salvation through Jesus' death and resurrection, but we find our worth and security in the knowledge of the Father's love. The blood of Jesus cleanses us from sin, and it is the love of the Father that brings us into wholeness.

"When my mother and my father have forsaken me, then the Lord will take care of me" (**Ps. 27:10**). The Lord can give us what our parents failed to give us, whether it is acceptance, encouragement, time, commitment, unconditional love, discipline, or blessing.

We need to see God the way that Jesus revealed Him in the Scriptures, not the way our human authority figures, our cultures, or our educational systems have represented Him to us. In verse 11, the first word David cries out to God in Hebrew is **Horeni**. The root of this word means 'to teach.' It comes from the Hebrew root word **horim**, which means 'parents.' Parents are responsible to teach us the ways of God. David was saying to the Lord, "Teach me as a parent" or "Parent me!"

Suggestions for prayer

The main key for releasing past pain is to forgive those who have hurt you. Forgive your parents, guardians, and/or other significant authorities. Then in prayer, separate your concept of God from their representation.

Confess your sin of judging authorities and reacting to them in unloving ways. Receive the Lord's forgiveness. Release any expectations you have (had) of them that they have not fulfilled.

Repent for believing lies about God and for judging or accusing Him. Ask for His forgiveness.

Ask God to reveal to you Who He really is, especially as Father. Ask Him to fill the empty places in your heart with His love and to heal all wounded areas there.

THE FATHER HEART OF GOD

Introduction

Have you ever wondered what God thinks of you? Is it hard for you to believe He loves you as much as the Bible says He does? Do you know anything about His emotions or His character?

One of the most wonderful revelations of the Bible is that God is our Father. What do you think of when you hear the word "father"? Do you think of protection, provision and tenderness? Or does the word "father" produce different kinds of pictures for you? God reveals Himself in the Bible as a gentle, forgiving Father, intimately involved with every detail of our lives. It is not only a beautiful picture, but a true one. However, most people have a different idea of what God is like. Each of us unconsciously tends to attach the impressions that we have of our earthly fathers to our concept of our Heavenly Father. Our experiences with human authorities usually influence how we relate to God. Good experiences bring us closer to knowing and understanding God, just as bad experiences create distorted pictures of God's love for us.

God intends the family unit to be a place where His love is demonstrated to both parent and child. As parents we begin to really understand God's heart towards us as His children. And as children, it is God's will that we experience His love through parental tenderness, mercy and discipline. But what if the ideal did not happen? What if one or both of your parents failed you? So many have suffered hurt and rejection by their families that it is hard for them to see God as He really is. Understanding the character of God is essential if we are to love Him, serve Him, and be like Him.

I want to talk about five areas of misconception concerning God and His love for us. I will be referring almost exclusively to God's qualities of fatherhood. However, a full revelation of God's parental love is incomplete without the presence of the female attributes of parental affection as well. *And God created man in His own image, in the image of God He created him; male and female He created them"* (**Gen. 1:27**).

Look back into your personal past and see if your relationship with God has been hindered in any way because of an absence of tender loving care from one or both of your parents.

I. Parental Authority

Have you ever gone to a friend's house and been greeted by the family dog? The dog will either cower away from you with fear, or leap upon you with excited affection. The puppy that fears trusting you has been mistreated. The exuberant loving dog has obviously come from a loving home.

In the same way, our past experiences dictate our responses when God reaches out to <u>us</u>. *"When Israel was a child I loved him, and out of Egypt I called My son. But the more I called Israel, the further they went from Me. They sacrificed to the Baals and they burned incense to images. It was I who taught Ephraim to walk, taking them by the arms; but they did not realize it was I who healed them. I led them with cords of human kindness' with ties of love; I lifted the yoke from their neck and bent down to feed them"* (**Hos. 11:1-4, Living Bible**).

Whose arms are big enough for all the lonely children of the world? Who weeps over our pains? Who will comfort us in our loneliness? ONLY GOD. Our problem is that we, like the abused puppy, shrink away from the One whom we assume will be like the other authorities in our life. But He is not—He is perfect love. He is gentle and long-suffering. He desires to show mercy and forgiveness. It was God who gave this command to parents in **Ephesians 6:4**: *"Parents do not keep on scolding and nagging your children, making them angry and resentful. Rather, bring them up with loving discipline the Lord Himself approves."*

II. Parental Faithfulness

God is consistently loving and faithful. Every promise He has made He will fulfill. You might want to trust Him, but deep in your heart you doubt His faithfulness. Do childhood memories of broken promises or neglect haunt you? Some of you screamed for hours as babies but nobody came to relieve you of your discomfort and hunger. Some of you wept behind locked doors, forgotten and alone.

Are you unable to sense His presence with you? Is your heart soft towards God or hardened with distrust? Hear His loving words to you. *"I will never desert you, nor will I ever forsake you"* (**Heb. 13:5**). Your Heavenly Father was there when you first walked as a child. He was there through your hurts and disappointments. He is with you now, at this moment. You were loaned to human parents who, for a few years, were to shower you with unconditional love. But you are and always will be a child of God, made in His image. Your loving Father waits for you with outstretched arms. What would keep you from Him? The God of Love still stands with open arms saying, *"I have come that you might have life and that more abundantly"* (**John 10:10**). *"Even when we are too weak to have any faith left, He remains faithful to us who are part of Himself, and He will always carry out His promises to us"* (**2 Tim. 2:13**).

III. Parental Generosity

The greatest demonstration of God's Fatherly heart seems to come with His attention to the details of our lives. He surprises us with those extra things, those little pleasures and treasures that only a father would know we yearn for. God is never stingy or possessive.

We tend to use people to get things; God uses things to bless people. We serve a generous God! The Psalmist said, *"Trust in the Lord and do good so you will dwell in the land and enjoy security. Take delight in the Lord and He will give you the desires of your heart"* (**Ps. 37:3-4**).

IV. Parental Attentiveness

There is one attribute of God that not even the best parent can hope to imitate—God's ability to be with you all the time. As parents we cannot provide constant attention 24 hours a day. We are finite beings who can only focus on one thing at a time. Not only is God with you all the time, but He also gives you His whole attention. *"Let Him have all your worries and cares, for He is always thinking about you and watching everything that concerns you"* (**1 Pet. 5:7**). God is constantly thinking loving thoughts towards you as though nobody else in the world exists. You say, "How does He do that? How can He be personally involved with billions of people at the same time?" It is no problem for the Creator of the world. Who knows how He does it? Just enjoy it!

You do not have to get His attention; He is already listening. Your parents were often preoccupied with their activities and sometimes showed little interest in the small events of your life, but God is not that way. He cares. Why does the Bible say that God has numbered the hairs of your head? He's trying to tell us in what detail He knows us and cares about our lives. Do not resent the failings of your human parents. They are just children who grew up and had children. Rather, rejoice in the wonderful love of your Father God.

V. Parental Acceptance

The kingdom of God is a kingdom of unconditional love. God's promises are conditional; that is, we receive the promises when we obey Him. But His love is unconditional. You do not have to wait to experience the love of God. Come as you are… Be honest with Him about your sin; He delights to forgive you because the blood of Jesus has already paid the price for all sin. Even in the depths of your past rebellion, He still loved you. Even God's judgments are motivated by love.

What is your response to God when He simply says He loves you? Can you receive His love without rushing into activity to earn His approval? One of the greatest pictures of peace and contentment is that of a baby asleep in the arms of a mother after having been fed. The child does not squirm and demand, he rests in the embrace of loving arms. The prophet Zephaniah described a similar emotion in the heart of God. *"He will save, He will rejoice over you with joy, He will rest in His love, He will joy over you with singing"* (**Zeph. 3:17**).

All through life you have had to perform and compete. Even as a baby you were compared with other babies, but God delighted in your uniqueness and still does. It is when you rest in the love of the Father that you cause Him to "rest in His love and joy over you with singing." Yes, there is much to be done in and through your life. There will be days when the Holy Spirit brings deep conviction of sin, showing you areas of your life that need to be changed and submitted to Him. But God is not always demanding changes. He knows our limits, and He gives us the grace and power to do the things He asks of us. He is compassionate. Most of the time He just says, "I love you" and softly speaks your name.

Conclusion

If you see that you have been hindered in your relationship with God due to some kind of failure of parental love, then take these things to the Lord. You must forgive from your heart anyone who has hurt you. If you do not, bitterness will consume you and you will find no peace with God.

Realize that you are not alone. There is no perfect person, nor a parent who has not made mistakes. Everyone has suffered hurt of some kind. One of the keys for release is found in forgiveness. The important thing is that you go forward and get to know God for who He really is—not who you think He is. He is the Perfect Parent. He always disciplines in love. He is faithful, generous, kind and just. He loves you and He longs to spend time with you. He wants you to receive His love and to know that you are special to Him.

(Used with permission by John Dawson, Founder of International Reconciliation Coalition)

EXERCISE #4 – THE NATURE OF THE SON

> ***Please Memorize:***
>
> **John 3:16-17** – *"For God so loved the world that He gave His only begotten Son, that whoever believes in Him should not perish but have everlasting life. For God did not send His Son into the world to condemn the world, but that the world through Him might be saved."*

* Pray for the vision of discipleship for yourself and for those in your group.

1. Jesus was both completely human and completely divine. The writer of Hebrews speaks of His divinity in Chapter 1. Read Hebrews 1 and then answer the following questions.

   The Lord's superiority to the angels is shown by what? (verses 4-6, 13-14)

   According to verse 3, what enables Jesus to reveal God?

   How does God address Jesus in Hebrews 1:10?

2. What did Jesus say about Himself in John 10:28-30?

3. Read Matthew 16:13-16. What did God reveal to Peter about Jesus?

4. Match the following Old Covenant Messianic prophesies with their fulfillment in the New Covenant, drawing a line from the promise to the fulfillment:

Micah 5:2	John 1:11
Isaiah 7:14	Acts 3:15
Zechariah 9:9	John 20:27
Psalm 16:10	John 12:13-15
Isaiah 53:3	Matthew 27:38
Isaiah 53:12	Matthew 1:18
Psalm 22:16	Matthew 2:1

5. How is the humanity of Jesus seen in the following situations?

    John 4:6 –

    John 4:7 –

    John 11:35 –

6. What did Jesus experience that is common to man? (Hebrews 2:10, 17-18)

7. What characterized the Lord's leadership? (Luke 22:25-27)

8. Read Romans 8:14-23. What will distinguish the sons of God?

9. Which of these traits are you exhibiting as God's son or daughter?

10. Take time to pray for an increase of the traits that are lacking in your life.

#4 – THE NATURE OF THE SON

In this session we will look at being baptized in the name (nature, character) of the Son of God, Jesus. Read John 1:1-4, 10-18 and let the Lord speak His Truth to you as you read.

Jesus fulfilled Messianic prophecy

There are 322 prophesies in the Old Testament that speak of the Messiah—His birth, life, character, sufferings, death and resurrection. Here are eight of those 322 Messianic prophecies and where we find their fulfillment in the New Testament:

1) Born in Bethlehem - Micah 5:2 (700 B.C.)   Fulfilled in Matt. 2:1
2) Preceded by Messenger (John the Baptist) - Isaiah 40:3   Fulfilled in Matt. 3:1-2
3) Entered Jerusalem on a donkey - Zechariah 9:9 (500 B.C.)   Fulfilled in John 12:13-15
4) Betrayed by a friend - Psalm 41:9   Fulfilled in Matt. 26:49-50
5) Sold for 30 pieces of silver - Zechariah 11:12   Fulfilled in Matt. 26:15
6) Money thrown in Temple/price for Potter's Field - Zechariah 11:13   Fulfilled in Matt. 27:5,7
7) Silent before accusers - Isaiah 53:7   Fulfilled in Matt. 27:12-19
8) Crucified with sinners - Isaiah 53:12 (700 B.C.)   Fulfilled in Matt. 27:38

In his book, *Science Speaks*, Peter Stoner shows that for any man to fulfill just these 8 prophecies would be a coincidence ruled out by the science of probability—one in ten to the 17th power. It would be written this way: one chance in 100,000,000,000,000,000. For one man to fulfill 48 prophecies is one chance in 10 to the 157th power. To fulfill all 322 prophecies—only God could!

There are 29 prophecies that speak of the betrayal, trial, death and burial of the Messiah. They were spoken by different people during the years 1000-500 B.C. and were all literally fulfilled in Jesus in one 24-hour period of time.

Proofs that Jesus is the Messiah

There are three things that prove that Jesus is the Messiah: (1) the fulfillment of Messianic prophecy, (2) the historical fact of His resurrection, and (3) the impact of His life upon history and upon countless individuals around the world. Recognizing that Jesus is Messiah and Lord and the One we are to worship and model our lives after, let us look at His nature. We will begin with how the Lord described Himself while on earth: as humble and as a servant.

Jesus was humble

In **Matthew 11:29** Jesus says, *"Take My yoke and learn from Me, for I am gentle and humble in heart; and you shall find rest for your souls."* The most basic quality of true humility is the knowledge of our dependency upon God. To be humble is to be approachable and gentle. It is the opposite of being arrogant. A humble person yields to the will of another.

Isaiah 57:15 speaks of being contrite, which means to be crushed as small as powder. In that crushing, our stubbornness is broken, and we no longer resist God, His dealings, nor the circumstances or people that He places in our lives. The Lord loves to dwell with the humble; they are easy for Him to be with, because their hearts are fully yielded to Him.

Jesus was a servant

In **Matthew 20:28** Jesus said, *"I did not come to be served, but to serve, and to give My life as a ransom for many."* In **John 6:38** He said, *"For I have come down from heaven, not to do My own will, but the will of Him who sent Me."* And in **John 12:49-50** Jesus said, *"For I have not spoken on My own authority; but the Father Who sent Me gave Me a command, what I should say, and what I should speak...whatever I speak, just as the Father has told me, so I speak."*

In other words, Jesus said, "I'm not my own boss. The Father dictates to Me, and I only say and do as He directs." Jesus was submissive to His Father and was available to serve others. He was fully obedient to His Father—even to the point of death on a cross.

Jesus was a man of prayer

Jesus revealed his humility and dependence on God by the amount of time He spent in prayer. He made quality and quantity time with the Father His chief priority. All of His ministry and service to people was an overflow of His personal ministry to God in prayer. *"But He Himself would often slip away to the wilderness and pray"* (**Lk. 5:16**). He would often leave the crowds, His friends, and even His family to be with His Father. He preferred His Father's company to the company of anyone and everyone else. *"And in the early morning, while it was still dark, He arose and went out and departed to a lonely place, and was praying there"* (**Mk. 1:35**). *"And it came to pass in those days, that he went out to a mountain to pray, and continued all night in prayer to God"* (**Lk. 6:12**).

Jesus prayed before and after ministry

Jesus knew He needed to be with God before He ministered to anyone. Because Jesus only did what He saw His Father doing, He made sure He had quality time with God. In **John 5:19**, He said, *"Most assuredly I say unto you, the Son can do nothing of Himself, but what He sees the Father do; for whatever He does, the Son also does in like manner."* Jesus also knew that He needed to be in God's presence after ministry, as that is where He was strengthened and restored. *"And when He had sent the multitudes away, He went up on the mountain by Himself to pray"* (**Matt. 14:23a**).

After we have given of ourselves in ministry to others, we often feel depleted and empty. We are more vulnerable to temptation at this time, so we must be extra careful not to be seduced by pride, lust, and worldly pleasures. Listening to secular music or watching unclean TV programs when we are exhausted can give the enemy an open door. When we are empty, we absorb more easily what is around us—God's presence or the spirit of this world. After preaching or teaching, we would be wise to find time alone with God to pray and be restored in His presence.

One of the enemy's favorite tactics is to get us too busy to pray. In our busyness, we might do more, but we accomplish less, because we are active in our limited strength. When we are prayerless, we become powerless. We must make sure we spend enough time in prayer!

Jesus lived to please the Father

The people and their needs did not control the Lord. However, He had compassion for them and ministered to them according to the Father's will. In the same way, we need to have a heart to serve others, but we must not be driven to serve! We must be led by God's Spirit. There will always be those who want us to do things that God has not told us to do. Jesus was in that position, too. Read how He handled the expectations of people in Luke 4:40-44.

The people pressured Him to stay with them, but He insisted on doing what He knew God wanted Him to do. He knew His Father's will because He had spent time in prayer and listened to His instructions. Look at what Jesus is clearly showing us to do by His example and words: We are here to please the Father, NOT to fulfill everyone's expectations of us! We must do what the Father tells us to do. We must seek God's direction for our lives—in all things, big and small. We can ask, "Father, what are You doing that I can do with you? What is Your will for me today?"

"For am I now seeking the favor of men, or of God? Or am I striving to please men? If I were still trying to please men, I would not be a bondservant of Christ" (**Gal. 1:10**). Too often we seek to please men and then try to persuade God to bless our decisions and actions. We are doing the opposite of what we should be doing! We are to please Him and persuade others to please Him.

Obey the will of God as He reveals it to you. There will always be overwhelming needs, and you will not be able to meet them all. Jesus did not allow others to dictate to Him. His life was not dominated by the claims of men; it was surrendered to the claim of God.

Jesus was led by the Holy Spirit

"For as many as are led by the Spirit of God, they are the sons of God" (**Rom. 8:14**). A mark of a mature believer is that he or she is led by God's Spirit. Examine yourself: are you being led? Or are you driven by guilt, pressures from others, fear of failure or of rejection, or the need for man's approval? Beware of the need for recognition and of the temptation to perform for acceptance. Knowing when to say "no" is part of maturity! Do not over-commit yourself! Channel your anointing in the areas where God has called you; do not scatter it in many directions.

Because we live in a self-centered world, there will always be those who take advantage of us as we serve them. Sometimes the hurt we receive is part of suffering for the Lord's sake. At other times, we are guilty of not setting proper boundaries, and we need to be more open and communicative about our limitations in service. Whatever the reason for our being wounded, we must always walk in forgiveness and love, pursuing peace with all men. Having intimacy with the Lord is the key to overcoming hurt and being able to forgive. God's love can heal us, and enable us to continue to humbly serve others.

PARABLE ON LIFE

He saw people love each other. And he saw that all love made strenuous demands on the lovers. He saw love require sacrifice and self-denial. He saw love produce arguments and anguish, and he decided that it cost too much. So he decided not to diminish his life with love.

He saw people strive for distant and hazy goals. He saw men strive for success, and women strive for high ideals. And he saw that the striving was frequently mixed with disappointment. He saw the strong men fail. He saw it force people into pettiness. He saw that those who succeeded were sometimes those who had not earned the success. And he decided that it cost too much. He decided not to soil his life with striving.

He saw people serving others. He saw men give money to the poor and helpless. And he saw that the more they served, the faster the need grew. He saw ungrateful receivers turn against their serving friends. He decided not to soil his life with serving.

And when he died, he walked up to God and presented his life to Him. Undiminished, unmarred, and unsoiled, his life was clean from the filth of the world, and he presented it proudly saying, "This is my life."

And the great God said, "What life?"

THE WINNER'S CREED

People are unreasonable, illogical, and self-centered—love them anyway.

If you do good, people will accuse you of being selfish and having an ulterior motive—do good anyway.

If you are successful, you will win false friends and true enemies—succeed anyway.

Honesty and frankness make you vulnerable—be honest and frank anyway.

The good you do today will be forgotten tomorrow—do good anyway.

The biggest people with the biggest ideas can be shot down by the smallest people with the smallest minds—think big anyway.

People favor underdogs, but follow top dogs—fight for some underdogs anyway.

What you spend years building may be destroyed overnight—build anyway.

People really need help, but may attack you if you help them—help people anyway.

Give the world the best you have and you'll always get kicked in the teeth—give the world the best you've got anyway.

When you were born, you cried and the world rejoiced. Let the rest of your life be in such a fashion so that when you die, the world cries and you rejoice!

EXERCISE #5 – THE NATURE OF THE HOLY SPIRIT

* Pray for the vision of disciple-making and for those in your small group.

1. Generally speaking, what is the role of the Holy Spirit in the life of a believer?

2. How has the Holy Spirit changed your life?

3. In John 16:7, Jesus said His going away was to the advantage of the disciples. Why?

4. Read John 20:19-23, Luke 4:18-19, and Acts 1:8, 2:1-4. What is the difference between the Holy Spirit being within a believer and being upon (or released through) a believer?

5. Have you experienced the Baptism in the Holy Spirit? If so, when?

Be prepared to briefly share your experience of receiving this gift.

6. What are some of the blessings the Holy Spirit is to us, according to Romans 8:14-17, 26-27?

7. Read 2 Corinthians 13:14. What is meant by "the communion/fellowship of the Holy Spirit?"

In what ways can you increase or enhance your fellowship with God's Spirit?

8. What does it mean to walk in the power of the Holy Spirit?

9. Read Galatians 5:22-26. The fruit of the Spirit should be evident and growing in our lives. Take time to ask God to mature the Spirit's fruit in you.

#5 – THE NATURE OF THE HOLY SPIRIT

In Matthew 28:19, we are told to baptize those who believe in Jesus into the name, nature, character, and Person of the Holy Spirit. The Holy Spirit is the third Person of the Godhead. It was by His power that Jesus was raised from the dead (see Romans 8:11). Just as radically as He transformed the body of Jesus in His resurrection, so He wants to revolutionize our lives!

The Person of the Holy Spirit

Read John 16:7-14. Jesus said the Holy Spirit convicts the world of sin, righteousness, and judgment. He guides those who believe in Jesus into all truth. He will convict us of every area of our lives that is not holy. He will foretell of future events, and will always glorify Jesus. He does not desire to make a name for Himself; His emphasis is Jesus!

"The Helper, the Holy Spirit, whom the Father will send in My name, He will teach you all things, and bring to your remembrance all things that I said to you" (**John 14:26**). How wonderful to have living within us a Helper who teaches us all things and reminds us of what Jesus has said!

Turn to John 14:15-18 and read it carefully. In verse 15, Jesus says we are to prove our love for Him by keeping His commandments. He had given His disciples some serious and difficult commands, such as: *"Love your enemies!" "Do good to those who hate you." "Pray for those who spitefully use you." "Be merciful the same way your Father is merciful."* Jesus knew His disciples would need help to obey His commands, so He promised a Helper.

The Greek word translated 'helper' is **paraklete**. It literally means, "one called alongside to help." **Paraklete** has a seven-fold functional meaning: Comforter, Counselor, Strengthener, Standby, Advocate, Intercessor, and Helper.

When does the Holy Spirit take up residence in our lives? The moment we repent of our sin and turn toward God, asking Jesus to be our personal Savior and Lord, His Spirit is joined with our spirit and He moves into our hearts and lives.

The Promise of the Father

Read Acts 1:4-8. The Greek word, **dunamis**, is translated as 'power.' From it, we get the word "dynamite" in the English language. It is explosive (miraculous) power and sustaining power. The sustaining power of God enables us to function with joy while enduring very difficult situations.

The disciples had been commissioned to preach the gospel to everyone and to make disciples of all nations, but Jesus said, 'WAIT, don't go without the power! You cannot do this in your own strength! You need the anointing! Do not even start until you receive My **dunamis** (explosive, sustaining power)!'

These disciples were already born again. In John 20, Jesus had breathed on them and said, *"Receive the Holy Spirit."* (**John 20:22**). But now Jesus was speaking of something different. We can have the Holy Spirit residing within us without our being baptized in the Spirit.

The Person of the Holy Spirit is a gift to us: He enables us to understand the Word of God, convicts us of sin, and sensitizes our consciences. He pours God's love and joy into our hearts. He helps us to see life situations with an eternal perspective. But, the Promise of the Father that Jesus told His men to wait for was not another blessing for <u>them</u> as much as it was a baptism for service for the benefit of others! The baptism with the Holy Spirit empowers, equips, and anoints us to minister the life of Jesus. The Holy Spirit is a blessing to <u>us</u> while living IN us, but He is also a blessing to <u>many</u> when He is released THROUGH us.

Manifestations of the baptism with the Holy Spirit

Both the public ministry of Jesus and the public ministry of the early Church began with a life-changing encounter with the Holy Spirit. The power of the Spirit in Jesus' life authorized Him to preach the kingdom of God and to demonstrate the kingdom by healing the sick, casting out demons, and raising the dead. The same power and authority was given to the disciples in Acts 2. Jesus Christ is the prototype of the Spirit-filled, Spirit-empowered life. The Book of Acts tells of the disciples receiving what Jesus received in order to do what He did.

In Acts 2:1-4, we see how the Holy Spirit was first given. The disciples had been praying together for 10 days, waiting for the Promise of the Father. Suddenly, the Holy Spirit filled the place with the sound of a rushing, mighty wind! He settled upon each of them in the form of tongues of fire. As they were baptized with the Holy Spirit, they began to speak in unknown tongues, as the Spirit gave them the words.

A prayer language of tongues is a common way the Holy Spirit expresses Himself when He is fully released in life of a believer. In **Matthew 12:34b**, Jesus said, *"For out of the abundance of the heart the mouth speaks."* So, when the Holy Spirit fills and overflows our hearts, He will often release tongues and/or prophecy through our mouths.

The Holy Spirit upon us

Consider the analogy of a firecracker, which has the potential of making a powerful impact. But only when the potential is released through lighting it do we actually experience that power. As believers, we have the potential of dynamite power when the Holy Spirit lives within us, but until He comes upon us and is released through us, that power is contained.

In **Luke 4:18**, Jesus read from Isaiah 61, saying, *"The Spirit of the Lord is UPON Me to preach, to heal, to set captives free...."* Notice the preposition *"upon."* As the anointing of the Spirit comes upon us, He is released through us in power. Within us, the Holy Spirit blesses us and can touch others through us. But the release/empowering of the Spirit brings a fresh boldness to witness, a release of joy, and a baptism of love for others.

Also, the spiritual gifts (see 1 Cor. 12, Rom. 12, Eph. 4) become more available to us for serving others. Read John 7:37-39. The Spirit will flow out from us as rivers of living water (not a trickle or a stream, but rivers of water – like a dam breaking!). This is a fulfillment of **Isaiah 44:3**, which says, *"For I will pour water on him who is thirsty, and floods on the dry ground; I will pour My Spirit on your descendants, and My blessing on your offspring."*

Those of us who want to serve God are in the same situation as the early disciples. We hear and want to obey our Lord's commissions to preach the gospel and make disciples, and His words to us are the same that He spoke to His men then, "Don't even try to do what I've called you to do without the anointing and power of the Holy Spirit!"

The gift of unknown tongues

Some people have difficulty understanding the gift of tongues. They ask, "Why do we have to speak in tongues?" The answer is: we do not have to, we get to! It is a blessing to pray in the Spirit! It builds up our inner man, and tunes us with the Spirit of God so that our thoughts and prayers become synchronized with His. It is a powerful prayer tool. It also opens the door for us to move into the other gifts of the Holy Spirit more easily.

If Jesus can control our mouths, He can control every part of us. **James 3:2** says, *"If any man offend not in word, the same is a perfect man, and able also to bridle the whole body."* **Psalm 12:4** says, *"With our tongue we will prevail; our lips are our own; who is lord over us?"* Who is lord over us is revealed by who masters our tongue! He who controls the tongue is master of all else. It is as if Jesus says, "Give Me your tongue, and I will bridle your entire body." In Mark 16:17, Jesus said that those who believe will speak with new tongues.

Speaking in tongues is often controversial in the Church, particularly because of the pride element. Pride of intellect can keep one from speaking in a strange tongue, and pride of having the gift of tongues can offend those who do not have it. We need to understand that all gifts from God are undeserved and unearned; they are not reserved for those who reach certain spiritual heights. The Holy Spirit freely gives His gifts to equip and empower believers for service. Any gift that God considers worth giving is worth seeking after and receiving!

Difference between a prayer language and a gift of tongues for the Church

There is a difference between the prayer language of the Spirit and the gift of different kinds of tongues used for the building up of the Church. The basic difference is directional—who initiates the communication, and to whom is it directed?

The prayer language of tongues is from us to God. *"For he who speaks in a tongue does not speak to men but to God, for no one understands him; however, in the spirit he speaks mysteries...He who speaks in a tongue edifies himself, but he who prophesies edifies the church"* (**1 Cor. 14:2, 4**).

The gift of tongues is a language of the Spirit that aids us in prayer and praise. Because it is to God, it does not need interpretation. The Holy Spirit knows the heart and will of God, and can assist us in praying effectively. We never pray wrongly when praying in the Spirit!

The gift of different kinds of tongues is from God to us. (*see* 1 Cor. 12:10) It is a message from God to the church in tongues that must be interpreted so that believers can be edified.

The Holy Spirit must first reside within us before He can be released through us, but there is no need for a time lapse between salvation and the release of the Spirit. We can be baptized with the Holy Spirit right after we repent and believe in Jesus. The release of the Spirit is not getting more of Jesus; it is Jesus getting more of us! It involves a deeper consecration to Him, a surrendering to His service, and a further dying to the self-life so that Jesus can live through us in power and holiness.

The Baptism with the Spirit is for all believers

Read Acts 2:38-39. Being baptized with the Holy Spirit is important for all believers. We live in a world of deception, temptation, and evil. We need the power of the Holy Spirit and His gifts in our lives, and will even more so in the days to come.

The baptism with the Spirit is the beginning of a deeper and more powerful walk with Jesus. The same Spirit that was upon Jesus comes upon us, and as we spend time in His presence and in His Word, His anointing upon us grows.

To receive this gift from God

(1) Ask Jesus to baptize you with His Spirit (see Matt. 3:11).

(2) Renounce all involvement in the occult or false religions.

(3) Forgive anyone who has hurt or disappointed you.

(4) Repent of any known sins of omission, commission, or disposition.

(5) Ask for a fresh cleansing over your spirit, soul, and body with the powerful blood of Jesus.

(6) Receive this gift by faith, knowing the Lord wants to give it to you.

EXERCISE #6 – THE TRAITS OF A DISCIPLE

Please Memorize:

John 8:31-32 – *"Then Jesus said to those Jews who believed in Him, 'If you abide in My word, you are My disciples indeed. And you shall know the truth, and the truth shall make you free.'"*

John 13:34-35 – *"A new commandment I give to you that you love one another; as I have loved you, that you also love one another. By this all will know that you are My disciples, if you have love for one another."*

---

* Pray for the vision of disciple-making, for God's work in your life, and for those close to you.

1. According to John 8:31-32, what is the essence of true discipleship?

In practical terms, how do we do this?

2. Discipleship results in freedom. What are some things from which you have been freed?

3. Jesus said we are to love as He loves. What qualities should that love include?

How do you find the ability to love others like that?

4. Read John 15:1-10. Explain what it means to abide in Jesus and what the results will be if we do.

5. Read Luke 14:26-27 and rewrite verse 26 in your own words.

6. According to Matthew 5:23-24, Matthew 18:15-16, and Luke 17:3-4, how are we to handle damaged relationships?

7. Explain the difference between Jesus being in us (John 17:21) and our being in Him (John 15:4,7).

#6 – The Traits of a Disciple

One of the keys to being a disciple of Jesus is found in **John 8:31-32**: *"Then Jesus said to those Jews who believed in Him, 'If you abide in My word, you are My disciples indeed. And you shall know the truth, and the truth shall make you free.'"*

Discipleship...

... **begins with faith.** We believe and accept all that Jesus says as being 100% true, and we acknowledge that He is the Messiah and Lord of all. *"For with the heart one believes unto righteousness, and with the mouth confession is made unto salvation"* (**Rom. 10:10**).

... **means consistently abiding in the Scriptures** through reading, studying, and meditating on them. It is the process of the "Word becoming flesh" within us.

... **is based on the truth of Scripture.** God's Word is inspired by Him and can be trusted to reveal Him and His ways. *"All Scripture is given by inspiration of God, and is profitable for doctrine, for reproof, for correction, for instruction in righteousness, that the man of God may be complete, thoroughly equipped for every good work"* (**2 Tim. 3:16-17**).

... **results in freedom.** Freedom can be instantaneous or a process. We become free as we read and apply the Scriptures to our lives. His truth progressively makes us free. The opposite is also true: as we cease to abide in His Word, we begin to lose our freedoms and we enter into bondage.

Freedoms available in Jesus

(1) freedom from sin – God's Word tells us that sin consists of <u>doing wrong</u> and <u>not doing right</u>. *"To one who knows the right thing to do and does not do it, to him it is sin"* (**Jam. 4:17**). There are sins of omission, commission, and disposition. We need freedom from them all! The apostle Paul says we are called to liberty in Galatians 5:13. We are called to freedom from sin, and to love and serve others. We are forgiven because Jesus paid our penalty, and because of that, we have the responsibility to forgive others for their sins. Receiving and giving forgiveness is a key factor in our being free from sin. Jesus' blood not only cleansed us from sin, it also broke the power of sin over us! He IS our righteousness and our sanctification! *"But of Him you are in Christ Jesus, who became for us wisdom from God—and righteousness and sanctification and redemption..."* (**1 Cor. 1:30**).

Before we received God's salvation through the sacrifice of Jesus, we were doomed to sin—we had no choice. But now, in Jesus, whether or not we sin is our choice. We no longer have the excuse that our bloodline goes back to Adam. We are new creatures in Christ, according to 2 Cor. 5:17. **Romans 8:2** says, *"the law of the Spirit of life in Christ Jesus has made me free from the law of sin and death."* How wonderful to be free from sin!

(2) freedom from self-love – **2 Timothy 3:1-2** says, *"...in the last days difficult times will come. For men will be lovers of self, lovers of money, boastful, proud, arrogant..."* The first item mentioned is that men *"will be lovers of self."* As we abide in the Word of God, we become less obsessed with ourselves and more enraptured with Jesus. Hearing and receiving correction becomes easier because we want to change and become more like our Messiah and King, Jesus. We learn to graciously embrace humility, apologize, and ask for forgiveness. Serving and preferring others becomes a joy rather than a duty.

(3) freedom from fear – *"God has not given us a spirit of fear, but of power, of love, and of a sound mind"* (**2 Tim. 1:7**). The spirit of fear tries to intimidate us, to make us "shrink back." Fear causes us to think and believe the worst will happen! It shows us where we need more of the fear of God and where we need to trust Him more. As we believe and receive God's love for us, it creates a shield that fear cannot penetrate. *"There is no fear in love; but perfect love casts out fear, because fear involves torment. But he who fears has not been made perfect in love"* (**1 John 4:18**).

One of the most common fears man has is the fear of death (alongside the fear of pain and suffering). For believers, this can include dying to self. Many people fear relinquishing their rights to the Lord. ("What will God require of me? Will I have to be a missionary...stay single...?") When we die to self, we allow God the right to choose our way for us. As we grow in the fear of the Lord and worship Him only, other fears will fade. Author John Bevere wrote, *"If you desire the praise of man, you will fear man. If you fear man, you will serve him—for you will serve what you fear."*

(4) freedom from the need for man's approval – We all care about what other people think of us. One of our basic emotional needs is to be accepted. Fear of rejection often influences our decisions and can control our lives. However, as Jesus' disciples, we are to be concerned with what He thinks, not with what man thinks. Our chief concern should be to know God's will for us. The Apostle Paul said in **Galatians 1:10**, *"For do I now persuade men or God? Or do I seek to please men? For if I still pleased men, I would not be a bondservant of Christ."*

A disciple is committed to unconditional love for others

In **John 13:34** Jesus said, *"A new commandment I give to you that you love one another, as I have loved you, that you also love one another."* And in **John 15:12** He said, *"This is My commandment, that you love one another, just as I have loved you."* What is new about this commandment is that we are commanded to love others as Jesus loves them. The Jewish people had been told to love their neighbors as themselves, but Jesus took that command further when He said, "Love as I love!" How did Jesus love His disciples?

(1) with understanding – Jesus knew His disciples well. He knew everything there was to know about them—their moods, struggles, weaknesses, and strengths—and He still loved them. To understand others, we need to "stand under" their point of view. This means we need to humble ourselves to genuinely listen to them. Most misunderstandings arise from a refusal to hear one another. When we really listen, we begin to understand their motives, thoughts, and feelings.

When we get alongside them and try to see from their perspective, we encourage transparency and trust. Such openness binds us together in love. It is the cement of relationships. *"Through wisdom a house [relationship] is built; by understanding it is established"* (**Prov. 24:3**). *"Get wisdom! Get understanding! Wisdom is the principle thing; therefore get wisdom. And in all your getting, get understanding"* (**Prov. 4:5, 7**).

(2) with sacrifice – Jesus loved sacrificially. There was no limit to what His love would give or where it would go. Jesus knew that His love would lead Him to a cross, yet He was willing to go there. True love will often involve pain and demand a cross.

We love a person sacrificially when we do not consider our own happiness and good over his. When we choose relationships based on how they will benefit us, we show our selfishness, the opposite of sacrificial love. When a man courts a woman, he easily spends his time, energy, and money on her. Sacrifice is easy for the person who truly loves.

(3) with forgiveness – Jesus held nothing against His disciples, not even their painful denial and betrayal of Him. They were often difficult to be with, but Jesus continued to love them. There was no failure or offense that He did not forgive. Love that endures all must be built on forgiveness. In any deep and precious relationship, there will be situations when forgiveness is required.

Forgiveness is not based on feelings; it is a choice of our will. We receive forgiveness (from God and others) by faith, and we offer it to others by faith. We choose to let the past go. If we wait until we feel like forgiving to do so, we will never forgive because our flesh loves to hold onto hurt and anger. Part of dying to self is releasing all transgressions committed against us. We put them behind us just as God puts our sins behind His back (*see* Isaiah 38:17b). We choose never to hold the sin of others in front of us to examine or think about again.

Guidelines for forgiving

In **Luke 17:3** Jesus said, *"Take heed to yourselves. If your brother sins against you, rebuke him; and if he repents, forgive him."* If he sins against you, tell him! Give him a chance to repent and apologize. When we forgive superficially and do not properly deal with offenses, our relationships lack in quality and depth. They tend to be superficial with little trust level. We must love others enough to discuss problems openly. As Jesus' disciples, we are to be committed to reconciliation and restoration. Unity is our goal!

In **Matthew 18:15** Jesus said, *"If your brother sins against you, go and tell him his fault between you and him alone. If he hears you, you have gained your brother."* If your friend offends you, speak to him alone. Telling others before you tell him affects how they view him and hinders the reconciliation process. If you know someone has something against you, intentionally seek reconciliation with them. We are responsible to seek peace no matter who is at fault; whether we are the wounded party or the guilty one, we must seek peace! *"Therefore if you bring your gift to the altar, and there remember that your brother has something against you, leave your gift there before the altar, and go your way. First be reconciled to your brother, and then come and offer your gift"* (**Matt. 5:23-24**).

The cost of being Jesus' disciple

Read Luke 14:26-30, 33. Disciples are willing to forsake everything for Jesus. Their love for God exceeds their strongest love relationships on earth. The Lord needs to know whom He can count on to stay faithful to Him, so He tells His followers to count the cost of being His disciple.

From 2 Corinthians 2:14-16, we see that *a disciple*…

… *possesses an attitude of gratitude.* A disciple is thankful for even small things and expresses his thanks.

… *walks in victory.* The Lord's disciple manifests the Lord's victory through his surrendered lifestyle. He looks for Jesus' triumph in all situations.

… *is "in Christ."* After salvation, Jesus is in us; however, our challenge is to be IN HIM! Jesus in us is salvation; us in Him leads to sanctification. This consistent abiding in Him is also referred to as "the rest."

… *carries the fragrance of Jesus.* A disciple gives off the aroma of death to the self-willed nature and the aroma of new life in the Lord. He/she leaves a strong impression of Jesus everywhere!

EXERCISE #7 – A MATURE SON OF GOD

* Ask the Lord to give you His love for people and His burden for their salvation.

1. After reading Philippians 2:1-8, write out a definition of humility.

2. Read Exodus 21:1-6. What is the significance of the slave's ear being pierced to his master's door?

How does this apply to us as bondservants of Jesus? (2 Peter 1:1a, James 1:1)

3. According to Hebrews 12:7-12, what is God's motive and purpose in training us?

4. What is God's destiny for us, as is written in Romans 8:29?

5. Read 1 Corinthians 9:24-27 and 2 Timothy 2:1-5. How would you define a spiritual discipline?

What is its purpose?

Which of the following spiritual disciplines are strong in your walk with God? Write a note next to the disciplines where you are falling short. This evaluation is for your own benefit. Do not let the enemy condemn you, but listen for the Spirit to convict you where you need improvement.

Inward Disciplines

Meditation – pondering over and thinking about Scripture. Ps. 1:2, Josh. 1:8

Prayer – speaking to and listening to God. Mark 1:35

Fasting – sacrificing food or pleasures in order to seek God. Isa. 58:6

Study – searching the Scriptures with commentaries and Bible helps. 2 Tim. 2:15

Outward Disciplines

Simplicity – living simply and frugally for the purpose of using your resources to build God's kingdom. Matt. 6:19-20

Silence and Solitude – quietly being alone with God. Matt. 14:23

Submission – denying self for the sake of others; yielding to the authority of another. Phil. 2:3

Service – meeting the needs of others. Matt. 20:26b-28

Corporate Disciplines

Confession – sharing one's weaknesses, sins, or faults for prayer and healing. Jam. 5:16

Worship – expressing our love and adoration to God. Ps. 95:1, 2, 6

Guidance – seeking God as a family or congregation for corporate guidance. Acts 13:2

Celebration – expressing joyful worship through singing, dancing, shouting, and praise. Ps. 150

#7 – A MATURE SON OF GOD

When Jesus first called His disciples, He said, *"Follow Me."* To follow Jesus as His disciple means to be wholly devoted to Him, gladly following Him wherever He goes. As we walk closely with Jesus, we will become better acquainted with Him and learn to know His ways and will. We will hear His heart, and our hearts will begin to beat with His. What matters to Him will matter to us. We will move from being earthly-minded to being eternity-minded. As Jesus said in John 17:3, it is eternal life to know Him and the Father Who sent Him.

Read Hosea 6:3, 6. The Hebrew text says, *"Let us run after* [pursue, chase] *the knowledge of the Lord."* We are to diligently pursue an intimate knowledge of God! If we do, He will come to us as certain as the rain upon the earth. In verse 6, God says, *"I would rather you know Me than to sacrifice to Me."*

Read Jeremiah 9:23-24. To know God is to personally encounter Him and to learn of Him through the Scriptures. Knowing God will naturally result in our loving and trusting Him. As we yield to this One we love, we will be increasingly transformed into His likeness. The ultimate goal of a disciple is to become like his Master in all things.

God has predestined us to be like Jesus

"Let this mind be in you which was also in Christ Jesus" (**Phil. 2:5**). As the Lord's disciples, we are to let Jesus' way of thinking govern the way we think. We are to have the same attitudes and values that He has, and to see others as He does. That requires a lot of mind renewal, which comes as we read God's Word. This is a lifelong process! But the more we ingest the Scriptures through reading, studying, and meditating on them, the more our minds will be renewed and our patterns of believing, thinking, and understanding will be transformed. *"And do not be conformed to this world, but be transformed by the renewing of your mind, that you may prove what is that good and acceptable and perfect will of God"* (**Rom. 12:2**).

Jesus was a bondservant

Read Philippians 2:6-7. A bondservant was one who assigned his personal rights to the authority and will of another. He chose to use his talents and abilities for one master, choosing never to leave him to work for someone else. When a bondservant allowed his ear to be pierced to the door of his master's house, he was saying that he would listen for his master's voice above all other voices and serve only him (*see* Exo. 21:1-6). Jesus had that relationship with His Father. He listened for His voice, and willingly gave His obedience, devotion, and loyalty to Him.

To embrace the same level of surrender, we must yield our personal rights to God. This includes our right to defend ourselves, to be treated fairly, to be comfortable, and to have privacy. It means to seek God as to how to use our money, energies, and time, and to trust Him without reservation. As a bondservant, we listen for our Master's voice above every other voice; we quickly obey what He says.

Right or righteous?

A great hindrance to our demonstrating the Lord's righteousness is when we insist on our own rightness. Being right and being righteous are not always the same thing! We sin against love when we insist that we are right, and the other person is wrong. God is not as interested in our being right as He is in our being righteous! A righteous person will humble himself and pursue peace with the other person, rather than try to determine who is right and who is wrong.

In Isaiah 53:12b, it is said of the Messiah that He would pour out His soul unto death, be numbered with the transgressors, bear the sin of many, and make intercession for the transgressors. Jesus did just that! He was killed along with thieves, bore the sins of the world, and died in the place (interceded) of all transgressors. He was righteous, yet He was murdered as a transgressor. Did He demand to be released? Did He demand His rights? No, He poured out His soul to death as a bondservant of the Lord. It is painful to be unjustly accused, to be misunderstood, to be right yet regarded as wrong…but our response is to be like our Messiah's, Who for righteousness' sake, endured our punishment. *"When He was reviled, did not revile in return; when He suffered, He did not threaten, but committed Himself to Him Who judges righteously"* (**1 Pet. 2:23**). It is not so important that we always be right, but it is very important that we always be righteous.

Learning to obey God

Read Hebrews 5:8-9. Although Jesus was God's Son, He still had to learn obedience through what He suffered (endured). Jesus never sinned while He learned from His trials. He was perfect as a baby, perfect as a teenager, and perfect as a mature adult. Bible teacher and author, Bob Mumford, illustrates this concept like this: an acorn is perfect; an oak tree is perfected.

God desires for us to be obedient to Him just as Jesus was. The Greek word translated obedience literally means, "to hear under." To be obedient means to hear with a submissive heart to obey. We are to bring our lives under God's rule and submit to all that He says to us. Jesus learned obedience by listening to His Father with an attitude of full submission. He complied with everything His Father said. Jesus never failed as He learned obedience. We do not have to fail either; we can obey the first time we hear.

Spiritual disciplines

To bring us to a place of spiritual maturity, God often appoints to us trials customized just for us. This is His prerogative. There are other avenues of training that we can choose to engage in; these are called spiritual disciplines. A spiritual discipline is any regular spiritual activity that trains, strengthens, and equips us for God's use. It requires focus, practice, hard work, and endurance. Through spiritual disciplines, carnality is loosened from us, and our new life in Messiah matures. God's grace is free, but the disciplines require our determined effort.

Spiritual disciplines empower us to develop and manifest the fruit of the Spirit as found in Gal. 5:22-23. They free us from our slavery to selfishness, and help us live our lives as Jesus taught and modeled for us. They are God's means of making us receptive and pliable so that He can shape us for His glory. By themselves, these disciplines can do nothing; they are merely the tools by which God can work deeply in us. In embracing spiritual disciplines, we bring ourselves before the Lord, and position ourselves for His transforming work in our lives.

12 Common Spiritual Disciplines

Inward Disciplines

(1) Meditation – Psalm 1:2. To meditate on Scripture means to ponder it, to turn it over and over in our minds until it penetrates our souls. Meditating helps us to separate our minds from the confusion of the world around us and to focus on the Lord. As we contemplate His character and ways, we gain wisdom on how to become more like Him. Scriptural meditation is marinating and soaking in the Word; it is being saturated by it. Meditating on God's Word results in our becoming more like the Living Word, Jesus.

(2) Prayer – Matthew 6:6-13. Prayer is the deepest and highest work of the human spirit. Real prayer is life changing; it is the central avenue God uses to transform us. Our prayers should include listening to God as well as talking to Him. Author William Carey wrote, "Secret, fervent and believing prayer lies at the root of all personal godliness."

(3) Fasting – Matthew 6:16-18, Isaiah 58:6. Fasting is abstaining from food (or pleasure) in order to seek God. It is often a neglected discipline but one that God expects all of us to embrace. Even though fasting will result in physical benefits, success in prayer, supernatural power, and spiritual insights, these benefits must not be our main focus. Seeking after God Himself should be the center of our fasting. Regular fasting, when added to prayer, is very powerful.

(4) Study – 2 Timothy 2:15. Studying God's Word is the main way we replace old destructive thought patterns with new, life-giving ways of thinking. Besides allowing Scripture to explain Scripture as when using marginal cross-references and study Bibles, we can also use Bible dictionaries and commentaries, various translations of the Bible, and other Bible helps.

Outward Disciplines

(5) Simplicity – Matthew 6:19-20. The discipline of simplicity is choosing to live simply and frugally for the purpose of using our resources to build God's kingdom. If we live simply and share our finances and goods, we make it possible for others to simply live. We can rejoice in God's gracious provision, but we are not to covet material possessions or base our security on things or money. Storing our treasures in Heaven rather than on earth will keep us eternity-minded.

Points on simple living:

• Pray about major purchases.

• Buy things that are useful and practical rather than for the purpose of impressing others.

• Avoid buying to the point where you go into debt; do not buy every new advertised item. Develop contentment with what you have.

• Develop a habit of giving things away.

• Learn to enjoy things without owning them (e.g. nature, beach, parks, the library, etc.).

• Give away anything that distracts you from your main goal in life.

(6) Silence and Solitude – Matthew 14:23. Solitude is spending time alone with God in a private, secluded place without interruptions. When we are silent, we can hear God's voice more easily and clearly. Experiencing times of quiet solitude prepares us to be more meaningfully with others.

(7) Submission – Philippians 2:3. Submission is the discipline of preferring others and joyfully laying down our rights and desires for their good. It is also yielding to the leadership of another, and requires a heart attitude of humility.

(8) Service – Matthew 20:26b-28. The discipline of service is to meet the needs of others by serving them. By embracing lower forms of service, we are resisting the world's system of selfish ambition and promotion. True service encourages, strengthens, builds, and heals the community.

Corporate disciplines

(9) Confession – James 5:16. Confession is sharing weaknesses, sins, or faults for the purpose of prayer and healing. As the Lord's priests, we have the privilege of speaking words of forgiveness to those who confess their sins to us. When sin is kept in darkness, it maintains power over its victim. Once it is confessed and brought into the light, the stronghold is broken, and freedom is available.

(10) Worship – Psalm 95:1-6. We worship God because He is worthy. Our worship is a response to His greatness and His love toward us. We enter His gates with thanks, His courts with praise, and His throne room with worship. Worship is the main key to kingdom advancement.

(11) Guidance – Acts 13:2. Besides being led by God personally, sometimes we need to seek His guidance corporately as a couple, family, or congregation. We are interdependent, having different gifts that complement one another. No one can hear the whole counsel of God in isolation.

(12) Celebration – Ps. 149:3; 47:1, 5-7. In corporate gatherings, we celebrate God's goodness and rejoice together with dancing, singing, shouting, and praising God.

We can turn almost any activity into an opportunity to develop our spiritual lives. The more we embrace spiritual disciplines and partake of God's means of grace, the more we will walk in holiness and joy with Him. We must realize that a disciplined person is not simply someone who exercises many disciplines. It is someone who can do the right thing at the right time in the right way with the right spirit. A disciplined person chooses to live in God's presence and under His reign. He embraces God's kingdom and will. And when he walks through trials and painful circumstances, he listens to God with a submissive heart to obey, thus learning greater levels of obedience to his King. Thus, suffering is also an opportunity to develop a closer, mature walk with Jesus.

EXERCISE #8 – A ROYAL PRIEST UNTO GOD

> ***Please Memorize:***
>
> **1 Peter 2:9-10** – *"But you are a chosen generation, a royal priesthood, a holy nation, His own special people, that you may proclaim the praises of Him who called you out of darkness into His marvelous light; who once were not a people but are now the people of God, who had not obtained mercy but now have obtained mercy."*

* Do you have a vision for investing into the spiritual lives of others yet? Keep praying for it.

1. According to Exodus 19:3-6, what was God's desire for the sons of Israel?

2. What is God's calling on and desire for us in the New Covenant, according to 1 Peter 2:9-10 and Revelation 1:6; 5:9-10?

3. What does it mean to be a priest of the Lord?

4. Read Jeremiah 15:19. What is/are the requirement(s) for being the Lord's spokesperson?

What are some of the worthless things that the Holy Spirit wants to remove from your life? (A way of speaking? An area of conduct? A pattern of thought or belief?) Ask the Lord to speak with you about this and write down what He says.

5. Read Isaiah 50:4-5 and 55:2-3. How well do you hear the Lord? Are you actively listening for His voice throughout each day?

6. After reading Ephesians 4:25, 29-32, make a list of what should come out of our mouths and what should not. Take time to pray over each of these admonitions from the Lord.

#8 – A ROYAL PRIEST UNTO GOD

"Now therefore, if you will indeed obey My voice and keep My covenant, then you shall be a special treasure to Me above all people; for all the earth is Mine. And you shall be to Me a kingdom of priests and a holy nation" (**Ex. 19:5-6a**).

God has always wanted a priesthood—a people who are set apart for Him to commune with Him, worship Him, and be especially His. When the nation of Israel did not keep His covenant and fulfill their priestly position, the Levites were chosen to be priests. In the Renewed Covenant (New Testament), believers in Jesus also have this high calling. *"You also, as living stones, are being built up a spiritual house, a holy priesthood, to offer up spiritual sacrifices acceptable to God through Jesus Christ...you are a chosen generation, a royal priesthood, a holy nation, His own special people, that you may proclaim the praises of Him who called you out of darkness into His marvelous light"* (**1 Pet. 2:5, 9**).

Part of our maturity as disciples of Jesus is to function within our priestly calling. It is a privilege to be God's priest, but it is also an awesome responsibility! He expects commitment, holiness, and availability from those called into this position.

Priestly ministry

Notice the Lord's possessiveness of His priests in His use of the words 'Me' and 'My' in **Ezekiel 44:15-16**: *"But the priests, the Levites, the sons of Zadok, who kept charge of <u>My</u> sanctuary when the children of Israel went astray from <u>Me</u>, they shall come near <u>Me</u> to minister to <u>Me</u>; and they shall stand before <u>Me</u> to offer to <u>Me</u> the fat and the blood," says the Lord God. They shall enter <u>My</u> sanctuary, and they shall come near <u>My</u> table to minister to <u>Me</u>, and they shall keep <u>My</u> charge."*

The priestly ministry of the Old Covenant included praying, reading the Scriptures, giving sacrifices and offerings, and worshiping the Lord. These activities were acceptable and very precious to God. The ministry in the Holy Place (inner court) was to God alone, and the ministry in the outer court was to the people. As God's priesthood today, we are responsible to go to God for the people through prayer and intercession, and to go to the people for God through preaching, teaching, and exhortation. We are to minister to the Lord before we minister to others. Once we hear from Him in the inner court, we will have His words of life and instruction to give to His people.

The power of the words of a priest

There is a discipline in hearing before speaking that we need to develop as priests. *"He opens my ear and gives me a word for the weary..."* (**Isa. 50:4**). In order to speak the words of the Lord, we must hear them! One of the primary ways to revolutionize our speaking is to revolutionize our hearing. When we are actively hearing God (through the Scriptures and by the Holy Spirit), we will be able to speak His words to others.

"For the lips of the priest should keep knowledge, and people should seek the law from his mouth. For he is the messenger of the Lord of hosts" (**Mal. 2:7**). As a holy priesthood, we are responsible to speak knowledgeably about the Lord and His Word. We are His messengers, spokesmen for the Lord.

"The tongue of the righteous is choice silver; the heart of the wicked is worth little. The lips of the righteous feed many, but fools die for lack of wisdom" (**Prov. 10:20-21**). Ask yourself: Do my lips feed others? Am I worth listening to? The key to having valuable, life-giving things to say is to be filled with the Lord Himself! If we fill our lives with God, then what we say will be an overflow of His life within us. In **John 6:63** Jesus said, *"The words that I speak to you are spirit and they are life."* As disciples of Jesus, our testimony should be the same as His; our words should be Spirit-inspired, giving life to those who hear them.

The damage of careless words

To our shame, we often speak carelessly and recklessly. We do not always think before we speak. We make irresponsible, quick statements that show we have not regarded the consequences of what we say. Too often we say the wrong thing at the wrong time or even the right thing at the wrong time. People are usually hurt when our words contain sarcasm, teasing, empty promises, or attacks on another's behavior or character.

The opposite of speaking recklessly is speaking with discretion, which is the quality of being careful, tactful, and polite. The discreet know when to speak and when to be silent. Someone once said, "It is a wise head that has a still tongue." King Solomon wrote, *"He who has knowledge spares his words, and a man of understanding is of a calm spirit. Even a fool is counted wise when he holds his peace; when he shuts his lips, he is considered perceptive"* (**Prov. 17:27-28**).

Ecclesiastes 3:7b – *"... there is a time to keep silence and a time to speak."*
Job 13:5 – *"Oh, that you would be silent, and it would be to your wisdom!"*

Speak gently and kindly

Before we speak, we should ask ourselves, "Is it kind and true? Is it necessary to say?" We should also consider how we say things. It is important that we speak gently. Speaking with gentleness is characterized by a controlled, soft voice, a caring facial expression that communicates acceptance, and a kind and compassionate manner.

"She opens her mouth with wisdom, and on her tongue is the law of kindness" (**Prov. 31:26**). All of us (men and women alike) should open our mouths with wisdom, and the law of kindness should be on our tongues. Our words have the power to bless and to curse, to encourage and to discourage, to heal and to wound. When we open our mouths, we minister life or death. As the Lord's priests, we must use our words to build His people and His kingdom.

Words that give life

"The mouth of the righteous is a well of life" (**Prov. 10:11a**). What do we need to do in order for our words to minister life instead of death? We must make sure that what is inside our "wells" (hearts) is clean and pure! *"Out of the abundance of the heart the mouth speaks"* (**Matt. 12:34**).

In seeking a pure heart, we need to repent from such sins as lust, pride, fear, anger, and bitterness, and allow the Lord to touch the hurting places within us that react defensively and angrily. We must choose to forgive and not allow grievances to accumulate. Any pollutant within us will make its way out in our words and attitudes.

More sins of the tongue to confess and renounce

Lying – Truth and integrity are foundational in the life of a priest. We need to be the same on the outside as we are on the inside. We must mean what we say and say what we mean. *"Therefore, putting away lying, let each one of you speak truth with his neighbor, for we are members of one another"* (**Eph. 4:25**). Usually we lie to defend or promote ourselves; lying encourages selfishness. It includes exaggerations, false impressions, deceit and hypocrisy. Even silence is a form of lying when we allow others to believe an untruth or a wrong perception. **Ephesians 4:15a** (Amplified Bible) says, *"Let our lives lovingly express truth in all things—speaking truly, dealing truly, living truly…"*

Slander and Gossip – God's priests must refuse to indulge in the sins of slander and gossip. Both of these involve the open, intentional sharing of damaging information. Whether the information we share is true or not, if it damages another person, we sin when we share it.

Criticism – Read James 4:11. When we criticize, we take God's place as the Judge. This reveals a proud and self-righteous heart, one that says, "I would not do what you are doing." What should we do when we see one another's weaknesses and sins? Intercede! God wants us to give ourselves to prayer, not to criticism.

Complaining – Complaining shows we have not learned to be content. We may be unhappy with ourselves, situations, or the world in general. Because we are not content, we become irritable, negative, and bitter. *"Do all things without complaining and disputing"* (**Phil. 2:14**).

Glorify God with your tongue

Psalm 34:1 says, *"I will bless the Lord at all times; His praise shall continually be in my mouth."* When we really believe God cares for us, we will find it natural to praise Him. We can be confident that He is Lord over every area of our lives and that nothing can touch us without His permission.

When we have developed a level of intimacy with God, our minds will be set on eternal things. Our spirits will commune with Him throughout the day, and the overflow of that abiding relationship will positively affect our conversations. We will speak words of life—words that encourage, edify, inspire, and refresh. Our words will draw attention to the Lord and glorify Him.

This does not mean that we should never talk about seemingly trivial things. There is a time to talk about jobs, clothes, and the weather, but is that all we talk about? Do our thoughts and words revolve around our concerns and ourselves or are they centered on the Lord? Are we functioning as God's priests, always available to minister to Him and to others?

Guidelines for self-evaluation, confession and repentance

Are you guilty of _____?

— Speaking recklessly and carelessly
— Speaking harshly rather than gently and discreetly
— Criticizing or judging
— Lying
— Complaining
— Speaking evil of others

— Are there any heart issues that you need to bring before the Lord so that your "well" can be clean?
— Do your words give living water to others? Do they minister life and edify?
— Is your prayer life active and effective?
— Do you gladly give God the praise that is due Him?

EXERCISE #9 – A DISCIPLE'S FIRST LOVE

Please Memorize:

Psalm 16:8 – *"I have set the Lord always before me; because He is at my right hand I shall not be moved."*

Mark 12:30 – *"And you shall love the Lord your God with all your heart, with all your soul, with all your mind, and with all your strength. This is the first commandment."*

---

* Ask the Lord who you are to begin discipling.

1. What is your interpretation of Matthew 10:37, Luke 14:26, and Psalm 45:10-11?

2. Read Revelation 2:1-5. What did Jesus commend these believers for?

What did He rebuke them for?

What does "leaving one's first love" mean?

3. Below is a list of evidences that we have left our first love. As you prayerfully read through them, be open to the Holy Spirit's conviction, repenting when necessary. Take time to talk seriously to Jesus about your love for Him, asking Him to purify and increase it.

I know I have left my first love when …

…my delight in the Lord is no longer as great as my delight in someone else. Mark 12:30

…my soul does not long for times of rich fellowship in God's Word or in prayer. Psalm 42:1

…my thoughts during leisure moments do not reflect upon the Lord. Psalm 10:4, Isaiah 26:3

…I claim to be "only human" and easily give in to those things that I know displease the Lord.

…I view the commands of Jesus as restrictions to my life rather than expressions of my love.

…I inwardly strive for the praises of this world rather than the approval of the Lord. 1 John 2:15

…I fail to make Jesus or His words known because I fear rejection. John 15:20

…I am unable to forgive another for offending me. 1 John 4:20

4. Read Revelation 19:1-9. Who do you believe is the Lamb's Bride?

How does she make Herself ready?

#9 – A Disciple's First Love

"And you shall love the Lord your God with all your heart, with all your soul, with all your mind, and with all your strength. This is the first commandment" (**Mark 12:30**). A disciple of Jesus loves God with all that he is. All of his actions and choices are motivated by that fervent love. Because of it, he wants to be holy. He wants to keep God's commandments. He wants to make disciples and to serve the Lord. He is faithful to God in good times and in bad because he has chosen to set his affection on Him.

Jesus wants more intimacy with us than we have given Him. Too often we have loved Him at arms' length or with a divided heart. We have loved Him conveniently but not sacrificially. The Lord is looking for those whose hearts belong to Him, who love Him fully and without distraction. *"For the eyes of the Lord run to and fro throughout the whole earth, to show Himself strong on behalf of those whose heart is loyal to Him"* (**2 Chron. 16:9b**).

First love

Basilea Schlink, in her book, *Those Who Love Him*, describes a "first love" for Jesus this way:

> *"First love" is first-class love, that of greatest quality. This love has eyes for the bridegroom alone. He fills her every thought, her every moment; to Him goes the yearning of her heart. Bridal love is a spendthrift love, lavish love, doesn't-count-the-cost love. It is sacrificial love, giving everything to the Beloved. Compared to the Beloved, all else is empty and worthless. Bridal love has one dominant characteristic: it occupies itself exclusively with Jesus, is always available to Him, and finds complete fulfillment in Him.*

Read Revelation 2:1-5. Jesus commended the Ephesians for their good works, spiritual maturity, and faithfulness, but He reproved them for leaving their first love. Just as He said to the believers in Ephesus, so He is saying to many of us today: "It does not matter how mature you are in good works, how discerning you are, how faithful you have been...I have something against you! You have left your first love. You have left it while pursuing good works, and while serving people. You have left it as worldliness has crept into your heart and cooled your passion for Me. You do not love Me like you used to." Our love relationship with Jesus should be the chief motivating factor in our lives, and the inspiration behind all service we give to others.

Jesus calls us to Himself

In this last session, we will look at some verses in the book of Song of Songs (Song of Solomon). This book of the Bible can be interpreted in a few ways, one of which is as a figurative description of Jesus' love for us and our bridal-type love for Him.

"My beloved spoke and said to me, 'Rise up, my love, my fair one, and come away' " (**Song of Songs 2:10**). Just as the beloved calls his loved one to himself, so Jesus calls us to leave the distractions and demands of the world and spend quality time with Him. In **Song of Songs 2:14b** He says, *"Let me see your face, let me hear your voice; for your voice is sweet, and your face is lovely."* Hear Jesus say to you today: "I want to see YOUR face; I want to hear YOUR voice! Not just the choir of all voices, but YOUR voice. Not just a sea of faces, I'm looking for YOUR face!"

Read Song of Songs 5:2-6. In verse 2 we read that she was asleep but her heart was awake. Has your heart ever been so connected with someone that even when you were asleep, you were aware of that person? The Shulamite's heart was so in tune with her lover that she heard his voice even while she was sleeping. Is your heart in tune with your Master's voice? Are you spiritually alert even while you are working, studying, or resting?

Being available to God

He says, *"Open for me..."* This is a timely word for God's people today! Too many of us are not open for and available to the Lord! Many things distract us. It is as if Jesus were saying to us, "Let Me into your busy and crowded life."

"Behold, I stand at the door and knock. If anyone hears My voice and opens the door, I will come in to him and dine with him, and he with Me" (**Rev. 3:20**). This verse is often used in sharing the gospel with unbelievers, but Jesus was actually speaking to His own people when He asked to be allowed in for fellowship! Supper is often a quick meal, but dining includes many courses. Jesus wants to dine with us! He wants significant time with us, not just quick chats.

The Lord waits for us

Further in verse 2, he states that his hair is wet, covered with dew. He had been waiting outside long enough for the evening humidity to get his hair wet! He had not just arrived; he had been waiting (How often does the Lord have to wait for us to respond to Him?). The Shulamite heard her beloved calls to her, but she hesitated before responding to him. She had already washed her feet (from the dirt floors) and had dressed for bed. In order to let him in, she would have had to get up and dress, and then wash her feet again before returning to bed. It was inconvenient for her to respond. She wanted to be with him, but she was not willing to make the effort.

Today's believers are often like this concerning prayer. We want fellowship with God, but we do not want to be inconvenienced to gain it. We want to know His heart, but we are too busy or too tired to listen to Him. We hear God's call to intimacy (to watch and pray), but we are unwilling to make the effort. We do not want to get up early; we do not want to miss out on evening functions. We love to fellowship with one another, and we do not want to neglect that in order to fellowship with God. The truth is: we are unwilling to sacrifice in order to find God in the secret place.

The mark of His presence

"My beloved put his hand by the latch of the door, and my heart yearned for him" (**Song of Songs 5:4**). She saw his hand come by the latch of the door, reach through the small opening, and feel the handle of the lock. Finding the door locked, he left his perfumed oil on the latch and left. A locked door indicated that either no one was home or that it was an inconvenient time for a visitor.

In verse 5 we read that when she saw his hand, the love in her heart overcame her desire to stay in bed. She rushed to the door, but instead of finding him, she found only His oil of myrrh on the handle. According to the courting traditions of that day, if a man came to visit his lady friend and she was not at home, he would leave his perfumed oil on the door handle.

Myrrh was not an ordinary perfume. It signified sacrificial love, suffering, and death. It was often used in preparing a body for burial. The myrrh that he left was proof of his desire to be with her and of what it would cost her to have quality time with him. Although she saw his hand and felt the oil of his presence, she missed the intimate communion he wanted with her. It is as if he had invited her to embrace a form of death—death to self, to sleep, to convenience—in order to have intimate time with him, and she refused.

Fellowship with Jesus will cost us

As the beloved called the Shulamite to himself, so our Beloved Messiah calls us to be with Him. But choosing to be with Him is costly. If we want intimate fellowship with Jesus, it will cost us time and energy, comfort and convenience; it will cost us our lives. We must embrace death to self in order to receive the rich quality of life that only Jesus can give. For us to enjoy ongoing communion with Him we must embrace ongoing denial of self.

In Song of Songs 5:6 we see that she was not satisfied with just his fragrance; she wanted him, and she began to search for him. We need to learn from the Shulamite's mistake. When our Lord says, "Come away and be with Me," we must stop what we are doing and be with Him!

God wants our obedience

An American pastor heard God tell him to spend time in prayer one day, but he had planned to watch football on TV. So he told God that if he could watch the game, he would spend five hours in prayer afterward. God was silent, and he decided that meant it was okay for him to watch the game. Afterward he went into his prayer room and said, "Here I am, Lord, for prayer. What is on Your heart?" But Heaven was silent. The pastor spent the next five hours trying to hear from God, but he never felt His presence or heard His voice. He searched for God, but he did not find Him. The Holy Spirit had withdrawn. Finally, he repented of his disobedience and of grieving the Spirit, and he determined to obey God in the future. Obedience is better than sacrifice!

Today many of us in the Body of Christ are satisfied with the fragrance (the perfumed oil) of God without paying the price to have personal encounters with Him. We are content to be saved, but we do not care to know the depths of the Lord Jesus. We stop short of true intimacy because we do not want to embrace the death that is necessary to really know Him. (For example: we may feel the Lord's presence in a service and yet avoid personal contact with Him. Or we can sense God's presence in prayer, yet we can refuse to hear His voice by not actively listening to Him.)

Jesus wants to be our first love!

One of the greatest hindrances to our attaining genuine closeness with the Lord today is that we are content with less than what He has for us. We can enjoy the excitement of praise, the elation of spiritual warfare, and the warmth of worship, and yet we can still miss out on true heart-to-heart encounters with Jesus. We are having FAMILY time with Him with our brothers and sisters, but not personal time alone with Him. The Lord loves family time, but His heart longs for individual time with each one of us.

Let's not be satisfied with anything less than intimacy with Jesus! He is calling us all to come to Him! Some of us need to set aside other loves, interests, and priorities, and give Him our first love. Jesus is to be the One we love the most! He is looking for a people who sincerely want Him, those who are not content with just the fragrance of His presence.

CONCLUSION

Now that we have completed these sessions of the Vision for Discipleship, would you consider yourself a disciple? Are you growing into spiritual maturity, functioning in your priestly calling, and increasing in your fervent love for Jesus?

Have you caught God's vision for making disciples? Do you see the value of investing time and the Word of God into those who believe in Jesus as the Messiah?

If we all invested at least a year into the lives of new believers (or older believers who have not yet been discipled), teaching them God's Word and helping them grow in their faith, we would see great maturity come into the Body of Christ. The Lord is not looking for masses of converts who do not really know Him or serve Him. He is looking for committed disciples who obey Him as Lord and are living godly, holy lives.

Jesus has given commissions to all of us who are called by His name. Even though our lifestyles and callings may vary, we are still commanded to:

• Pray the Lord of the harvest to send laborers into His harvest fields.

• Preach the gospel to everyone, heal the sick, and cast out demons.

• Produce disciples by going into all nations and establishing believers in their relationship with the Lord. Immerse them into the knowledge and experience of God as Father, Son, and Holy Spirit. Then teach them the culture of God's kingdom—His commands given to us in His Word.

Everyone should have the opportunity to know and love the Lord as we do! St. Augustine (354–430 A.D.), Bishop of Hippo, wrote: *"To fall in love with God is the greatest of all romances; to seek Him, the greatest adventure; to find Him, the greatest human achievement."*

PERSONAL EVALUATION

1. How has this study affected your perspective and attitude about being a disciple of Jesus?

2. What has it cost you to submit to Jesus as His disciple?

3. What changes in your personal life and/or walk with God have you experienced since you became a part of a small discipleship group?

4. What do you feel the Lord is saying to you about strategic disciple making?

5. Are you ready to invest into the lives of others through discipling? If so, how do you intend to go about that?

BIBLIOGRAPHY

Amplified Bible (The Lockman Foundation, 1987).

Bevere, John, *Breaking Intimidation* (Orlando, FL: Creation House, 1995).

Chambers, Oswald, *My Utmost for His Highest* (New York: Dodd, Mead and Company, Inc., 1935).

Dawson, John, *The Father Heart of God* (Tyler, TX: Wise Tracts, Last Days Ministries, 1981, 1994).

Eims, Leroy, *The Lost Art of Disciple Making* (Colorado Springs, CO: Navpress, 1978).

Foster, Richard J., *Celebration of Discipline* (New York, NY: Harper & Row Publisher, Inc., 1978).

Green, Keith, *"Jesus Commands us to Go"* (song) from Volume II, The Ministry Years, 1980-82.

Hill, Gary, *The Discovery Bible* (La Habra, CA: The Lockman Foundation, 1987).

Joyner, Rick, *The Harvest Volume II* (Charlotte, NC: MorningStar Publications, 1994).

Mayhall, Carole, *Words that Hurt Words that Heal* (Colorado Springs, CO: Navpress, 1990).

McClung, Floyd, Jr., *The Father Heart of God* (Eugene, OR: Harvest House Publishers, 1985).

MacDonald, Gordon, *Restoring your Spiritual Passion* (East Sussex, England: Highland Books, 1987).

McDowell, Josh, *Evidence that Demands a Verdict* (San Bernardino, CA: Here's Life Publishers, Inc., 1979).

New American Standard Bible (The Lockman Foundation 1962, 1963, 1968, 1971, 1973, 1974, 1977).

New King James Bible (Thomas Nelson, Inc. 1979, 1980, 1982).

Peterson, Eugene H., *The Message* (Colorado Springs, CO: Navpress, 1995).

Schlink, Basilea, *Those Who Love Him*, (UK: Zondervan Publishing House, 1969).

Spirit Filled Life Bible (Nashville, TN: Thomas Nelson Publishers, 1991).

Thompson, Dr. Bruce, *Walls of my Heart* (Euclid, MN: Crown Ministries International, 1989).

Tozer, A.W., *That Incredible Christian* (Harrisburg, PA: Christian Publications, Inc., 1964).

Made in the USA
Monee, IL
27 October 2020